Letters from
the Pacific

Letters from the Pacific

A Combat Chaplain in World War II

RUSSELL CARTWRIGHT STROUP

Edited with an Introduction by
RICHARD CARTWRIGHT AUSTIN

University of Missouri Press
COLUMBIA AND LONDON

Library of Congress Cataloging-in-Publication Data

Stroup, Russell Cartwright, 1905–1977.
    Letters from the Pacific : a combat chaplain in World War II /
Russell Cartwright Stroup ; edited with an introduction by Richard
Cartwright Austin.
        p.   cm.
    ISBN 0-8262-1288-3 (alk. paper)
    1. Stroup, Russell Cartwright, 1905–1977—Correspondence.
2. World War, 1939–1945—Campaigns—Pacific Area.   3. World
War, 1939–1945—Personal narratives, American.   4. United
States. Army—Chaplains—Correspondence.   5. World War,
1939–1945—Chaplains—United States—Correspondence.
6. Chaplains, Military—United States—Correspondence.
I. Austin, Richard Cartwright, 1934–   II. Title.
D767.S783 2000
940.54'78'092—dc21
    [B]   99-085994

Designer: Elizabeth K. Young
Typesetter: BookComp, Inc.
Printer and binder: Edwards Brothers, Inc.
Typefaces: Bodoni BE Condensed, ITC Giovanni

Dedicated to

Gerald Norwood, Paris, Texas

Frank E. McCann

Warren R. Corn, Willow Springs, Missouri

Frank Deshazer, Scotts Bluff, Nebraska

Roy W. Stemple, Aurora, West Virginia

Joseph P. Gloeckel

Roy Vance, Houlka, Mississippi

Joseph Ballard, Kansas City, Missouri

Andreas Zimmerman, Union City, New Jersey

Raymond Bouvia, Pocatello, Idaho

Lloyd Nedved, Tyndall, South Dakota

Walter F. Roseberry, Wichita, Kansas

Roy M. Smith, Athens, Alabama

Carl H. Norlin, Alta, Iowa

Daniel S. LaShille

These died in battle in the Cabaruan Hills, Philippines,
January 27 to 29, 1945.
Many were brought in from the field, and all were buried,
by Chaplain Russell Cartwright Stroup.

*"There was no wounded man who did not receive
spiritual comfort from the chaplain,
and there was no dead body which was not recovered,
in spite of danger and difficulty."*

Contents

Letters from
the Pacific

Introduction

In 1942, Russell Cartwright Stroup was thirty-seven years old and restless. He remained unmarried, the sole support for his mother, Emma, and his older brother, Cranston, both of whom lived with him. Emma walked with crutches, having lost one leg, when Russell was nine years old, in an automobile accident that also took the life of Russell's father. Cranston, once a recognized poet, was now stricken with encephalitis, a brain disease that prevented him from writing or teaching.

After graduating from Stanford University and reading for the Methodist ministry, Russell Stroup (pronounced Strowp) had undertaken two pastorates in southern California. Now he was minister to the First Presbyterian Church in the small southern city of Lynchburg, Virginia. An excellent preacher and attentive pastor, Stroup was beloved by his parishioners, even though they were southern and conservative while he was neither.

While a student, Stroup had been a peace activist and a pacifist critic of the First World War. Now the Second World War raged. This time he saw a sharper demarcation between those who fought to impose tyranny and those who fought to defend liberty. He did not believe that good could come from warfare, but he began to think that this war was necessary to resist the spread of evil. He was determined that he would not carry a weapon or kill another human being. Yet perhaps he could serve those who must do so. Most American men his age and younger would be shaped by their experiences in this war. Could he, afterward, continue as their pastor if he had not shared their risks and their sacrifices? Convinced that he could not, he decided to enlist as a chaplain in the United States Army and to serve, if possible, with infantrymen in combat.

In New Guinea and in the Philippines, Stroup volunteered to accompany one beachhead invasion after another, and to join troops

1

probing behind enemy lines. He fought postcombat depression. He tried to reassure his anxious family at home and to justify his repeated choice to place himself at risk. He offered encouragement to inexperienced and fearful troops, while restraining those tempted to abuse enemy prisoners. His transparent faith, and his willingness to place himself in harm's way, inspired soldiers in combat and comforted the wounded and the dying.

Stroup poured his observations and his feelings into frequent letters home, deliberately creating a deposit against the day he might find leisure to return to this material for reflection and further writing. The letters record a remarkable search for meaning and for purpose in the midst of combat.

Russell Stroup had grown up in East Cleveland, Ohio, the child of Ner Wallace Stroup, an unusually gifted Methodist minister, and Emma Cartwright Stroup, an outspoken Methodist evangelist and suffragist. In a letter from the Pacific theater, Stroup reflected upon his childhood.

> The first ten [years] were just about perfect. I couldn't have chosen a better family to be born into or better home influences. I had the finest mother and father in the world and an eminently satisfactory brother and sister. We had a well-rounded life that comes to too few children. There was discipline without harshness and love without sentimentality. We had plenty of healthful out-of-doors recreation and a large measure of mental stimulation and guidance. My tastes were formed along the right lines, and everything was done to make me happy. I was supremely happy. I remember those years vividly and I remember nothing but pleasure and purposeful growth. The splendid physique I was given, I still enjoy. The mental tastes I acquired are my constant delight. The spiritual foundations that were laid have been my abiding support. It was in those years that I learned tolerance, love of fair play, delight in the true and the beautiful, a sense of my personal responsibility, an unshakable Faith in which there was little of bigotry, a deep love of my Country combined with a feeling for other nations. In short, it was to those years that I owe whatever good I have.

In fact the idyllic childhood that Stroup recalled ended abruptly in the middle of his tenth year. He was riding in the backseat of the family car with his older brother, Cranston, and his younger sister, Margretta, when a traffic light forced his father to stop atop the interurban trolley tracks that crossed the highway. As a trolley approached, its brakes failed. The *Cleveland Plain Dealer* for Monday, July 20, 1914, reported:

> The auto was struck squarely in the center by a westbound [trolley] car. The machine was catapulted into the air and, as it struck, was carried by the interurban twenty feet along the track, when it overturned and almost at once began to blaze.

The children were thrown free, but their parents were trapped in the wreckage. A week later their father died in the hospital from his burns at the same time that their mother was in surgery for the removal of her left leg. After many skin grafts and nine months in the hospital, Emma returned to her children. She walked with crutches for the remainder of her ninety-five years.

A woman both spiritual and resourceful, Emma began her new life as a single parent with no more than the house she owned and a small widow's pension from the Methodist Church. After selling her house, she supported her family by purchasing and occupying a smaller house needing renovation, supervising the renovations, then selling that house to purchase another.

For a few months in 1916, when he was eleven years old, Russell kept a diary. In one entry he wrote, "Mama is thinking of sending Cranston and myself to some boys camp where we can be with fine manly men. It is so much like her. Every privation we have she tries and usually succeeds in making up for it a little."

Russell was an exuberant, sometimes mischievous boy. "We went to Sunday school and I hit a boy with a book because he shot spit balls in a rubber [band] and hit me several times. I expect trouble tomorrow." But he hated bullying. "I saw some boys mistreating a little boy and I made them stop. If it's anything I hate it's a bully. I see them a lot and if possible give them some of their medicine."

Even at the age of eleven, Russell had ambitions as a writer and submitted an essay to a children's magazine. "The contest in The American Boy closes Friday and I'm all aflutter about it. I keep wondering whether I'll get a prize." He didn't then, but he won a very practical prize for his writing twenty years later. In the midst of the Great Depression, Stroup moved his family from California to a small farm in Virginia where they struggled to survive with few resources. He bought a team of mules for plowing but could not afford other livestock. However, a farming magazine held a contest for farmers on the best method of raising hogs: the winner would receive a prize pregnant sow. Stroup, who had never farmed before, sped to the library at Washington and Lee University, read everything there about hogs, wrote an engaging essay, and won the prize. The ensuing litter of twelve helped the family to survive.

In 1918, after protracted litigation and two jury trials, Emma received from the interurban railway company a $55,000 settlement—a large sum at that time. Her wounds had been aggravated by the damp air of Cleveland. Now that she could afford to move a dry climate, she selected Pasadena in southern California.

The young boy who was able to knock down a bully would, in a few years, consider himself a pacifist. Emma had German heritage, and she was also a Christian Socialist. She made a practice of stimulating conversations around the dinner table on religious, cultural, and political topics. During the First World War, when Russell was entering adolescence, these conversations focused on a socialist and pacifist critique of American participation in the conflict—"a rich man's war but a poor man's fight." A family hero at the time was Herbert Hoover, the Quaker who organized relief efforts to sustain European civilians in combat areas.

Later the whole family moved north to Palo Alto so that the three children could attend Stanford University and still care for their crippled mother. Stroup studied history and political science. From 1920 to 1925, the years Stroup attended college, Americans were exuberant over their military victory in Europe but frightened of communists in Russia and of socialists at home. Stroup's convictions were considered suspect. He summarized his college experience in the reflective letter from the Pacific theater quoted above.

> In many ways I am not satisfied with our choice of college and yet we could have done much worse. I got a lot out of it, and that in spite of regrettable experiences there—which were still experiences. Maybe my best education came from my fierce reaction against the injustice and brutality of Stanford. There I learned that there are things to stand against and oppose with courage.

For a year following college he attended Drew Theological Seminary, where his father had been valedictorian. However, Drew now lacked intellectual challenge for Stroup, and he decided to read for the Methodist ministry on his own. He served two Methodist parishes in southern California, from 1927 to 1934. During his second assignment, in the midst of the Great Depression, Stroup helped the "muckraking" author Upton Sinclair to organize food bartering networks among poor farmers, unemployed fishermen, and migrant families who had fled to California from the Dust Bowl states. When Sinclair, a lifelong socialist, became a Democrat in order to run for governor, Stroup joined his upstart ticket in an unsuccessful bid for a seat in the U.S. Congress. Not long after, he felt that his opportunities for advancement in southern California were blocked. With his mother and brother, Stroup moved east to Virginia. After farming for several years, he was called to pastor the First Presbyterian Church in Lynchburg, at that time the most prominent church in the small city.

Stroup—handsome, witty, and intelligent—was very attractive to women, but his search for romance was inhibited by several factors. His religious convictions encouraged celibacy outside marriage. He was dissatisfied with any potential partner who could not be an intellectual companion. And he was, by the mid-1930s, the principal source of financial and emotional support for an invalid mother with a strong personality and a brother whose brain and nervous system were continuing to deteriorate from the effects of encephalitis.

In 1947, a year following his discharge from the army, Stroup married Louise Wells Baker, whom he met following his return to the States. Louise had been a founding editor of *Fortune* magazine and subsequently served as a special assistant to Henry Luce, the chairman of Time, Inc. They were in their early forties, and their eagerness for a child was soon rewarded by the birth of Susan Margretta. In 1950 Stroup was called to pastor the Georgetown Presbyterian Church in Washington, D.C., where my mother, Margretta, and I had attended for several years. This was the oldest congregation in Washington, D.C., a declining group in a reviving neighborhood. Stroup oversaw the restoration of the building and the revitalization of the congregation. His preaching, both spiritual and intellectual, drew government and professional leaders into a congregation that thrived until his retirement in 1970. Tragically, the Stroups' daughter, Susan, died of leukemia in 1956, just short of her eighth birthday. Her mother never recovered from this loss.

When Stroup retired in 1970, he was eager to resume writing and to begin teaching, but exhaustion and poor health prevented him. He died of prostate cancer in 1977. Years earlier he had lectured frequently at Washington and Lee University in Lexington, Virginia. When Washington and Lee awarded him an honorary Doctor of Divinity degree in 1947, the citation was apt.

RUSSELL CARTWRIGHT STROUP
You have been endowed with uncommon capacities of mind
and with compulsive powers of utterance;
you have vision of the vast need of the world
and you have tender awareness of the problems of a tortured
    human heart;
in the wide opportunities of peace and in the crises of war,
you move before men with a winsome influence,
and you devote your magnificent talents to the task
of bringing souls into the abundant life,
which is the way of Christ.

When I was nine years old, and then ten, my mother and I would drive the two hundred miles from Washington, D.C., to Lynchburg to visit my grandmother Emma and my uncle Cranston as frequently as gas rationing would allow. My father was in Italy with an army military-government unit. My mother worked, from the Pentagon, on the organization of civilians for "civil defense." In Lynchburg, Emma read aloud from my Uncle Russell's most recent letters. Together we shared the suspense, the excitement, and the sadness that they conveyed.

Yet, after the war, as our lives moved in other directions, this correspondence fell from memory. Stroup, busy with new challenges in his pastoral ministry, did not pursue his intention to edit the letters. Eventually they were stored away in the house he built for his retirement. When Stroup died in 1977, Louise invited her widowed sister, Marie, to join her in that house. When Louise died in 1981, Marie continued to live in the home and made few changes. Only after she died in 1994 did her son, Jeff Price, begin to systematically sort through the possessions of all three. The next year Jeff found most of Stroup's South Pacific letters and gave them to me; he found additional letters in 1998. As I read the letters, marveling at their vitality, I resolved to fulfill my uncle's intention and to edit them for publication.

Stroup could tell a good story. He was an introvert with a brilliant yet brooding mind and a keen sense of empathy. He had a love of words and a gift for language. Whether he was offering comfort or recounting an adventure, apt phrases seemed to emerge graciously as if by immediate inspiration. His sense of humor was sharp, often sardonic.

Because Stroup's combat duties required him to write many letters to the families of the wounded and the dead, he arranged to carry a small, portable typewriter with him almost everywhere. When his typewriter caught up with him four days after the Philippine landing, Stroup wrote, "This is, so far as I know, the only typewriter this far forward in the U.S. Army." During twelve months in combat he wrote hundreds of letters, an article for *Harper's Magazine,* and a series of articles for a church journal, the *Presbyterian Outlook.*

In his letters long sentences poured forth devoid of punctuation until the period at the end. The type crowded page after page. Most of these letters were written in haste, yet rarely was there a correction or a cross-out. Stroup loved to write, and once he began the words flowed freely.

The letters are not naive. Stroup stated that he was sending home accounts of his experiences and the thoughts of his heart so they might be kept safe until he could edit them upon his return. Much of his prose is a first draft with an eye to publication.

The letters had to pass U.S. Army censorship. Stroup could not reveal his location, but he became skilled at writing around army restrictions and thus managed to reveal almost everything else. In none of the letters preserved has a single word been blacked out or cut by an army censor. Furthermore, Stroup was conscious that his mother was his first reader. In some respects this encouraged frankness, for she was a brave woman with insight and compassion. Yet he chose to respect some of her conventions: he did not, for example, quote a swear word. Occasionally he placed stronger material in a letter addressed to his brother, even though he knew that his mother would eventually read that also.

In addition to the letters, two helpful items have survived. One is a pocket notebook from Stroup's final assignment in the Philippines. There, for his own interest, he listed the locations where he had served. The second is a one-page "Record of Service," listing his unit assignments and his combat landings, that Russell prepared many years later, perhaps to secure an Army Reserve pension. With these aids, with internal evidence from the letters themselves, and with available histories of the Pacific campaigns, it has not been difficult to locate events and to furnish appropriate context.

In editing these letters I have removed half the bulk, for some are repetitive, and some are of little interest beyond the immediate time or the immediate family. I have retained personal and family material that reveals Stroup's mind and heart. For the sake of clarity, I have standardized punctuation and usage to the extent that I feel Stroup would have in preparing these letters for publication, while maintaining as much as possible of his free-flowing style. I have written out abbreviations. I use an ellipsis to indicate when I have passed over a body of material, but I do not use one where I drop redundant words or sentences within a continuing narrative.

The originals of these letters and all other family materials utilized in the preparation of this book have been deposited with the Stroup Family Papers at the Western Reserve Historical Society in Cleveland, Ohio.

My Uncle Russell was a father to my youth and a beloved mentor throughout many years we shared together. I owe him life. To recover these letters and to rekindle his spirit has been a joyful opportunity.

1

"Our Chapel Has Been the Most Outstanding on the Fort"

On August 20, 1942, Russell Stroup was commissioned a first lieutenant in the Chaplain's Corps and enrolled in the Chaplaincy School at Harvard University. After a month's orientation to this profession, he was dispatched to the 100th Infantry Division, a new unit about to be established at Fort Jackson, South Carolina. There, after two weeks of additional orientation, Stroup was assigned to the 399th Infantry Regiment within the forming division. After a month's work assisting commissioned and noncommissioned officers with preparations for the arrival of soldiers, Stroup received his first commendation.

November 12, 1942

TO: Chaplain (1st Lt.) R. C. Stroup

For the hard work done and the excellent spirit evidenced by you during the "cadre" period of this regiment, I, as your Commanding Officer, desire to commend you. . . .

(signed) Andrew C. Tychsen
Colonel, 399th Infantry
Commanding

Although we do not know what efforts prompted this praise, the first of Stroup's letters that has been preserved tells of a crisis of morale among the recently assembled officers.

Tuesday, December 1, 1942

Dearest family,

The Christmas question has been settled by higher authority. We received our orders last night that all leaves had been canceled and that no one would be allowed to go home. The reason is that our men have begun to arrive and we reach our peak of reception on December 15.

The orders cast a black pall on the entire command. There was the man who planned to get married; there was another who planned to propose to his girl; there were men who had not been home for a year—many, many problems. A movement started among the noncommissioned officers to all go out and get drunk as a protest and as a release. To head this off I had to speak to groups and to individuals far into the night last night. Today is payday, which increases the problem. There is much left to do tonight.

To get back to Christmas: Since no man will be away and since we will have a host of new men just getting adjusted to things, it will be up to me as chaplain to provide Christmas for them. I'll try to make up for home and all the rest, and that won't be easy, but necessary. So if you and I aren't together for Christmas, at least we can feel that, through what we give up, others will have something of a Christmas. That may give us the best Christmas of all.

Russell

Once this crisis of morale was past, Stroup could review events with humor.

Saturday, December 26, 1942

Dearest family,

Now that The Day is over I can put the events of the week all in one letter. On the Sunday before Christmas we had a rather special service and better-than-ordinary music, along with fancy programs and decorations. To make the service more outstanding the general was gracious enough to drop in as he has threatened to do before without making good. Everyone was, in the quaint army custom, thrilled by his presence—although of course the chaplain paid him no mind. The general liked the service well enough to compliment me, which might be expected, but also well enough to make a glowing report to the division chaplain and, from reports that filtered down to me, to everyone else. That was nice.

Monday evening I stepped out into high society. The general had left a message for me to call a Mrs. T. in town. She invited me to join her friend, General Burress, and four other people to a dinner party followed by a "coming out" party for some gal at a local hotel. I accepted with pleasure, and she said that she would "tell Pinkie to call around and pick me up on his way down." I made some feeble protest about generals not picking up lieutenants, but she was adamant and I have learned not to argue with a lady.

The general arrived in the official Packard with his driver, and we were off. I found him quite pleasant to talk with and better informed about things than I had anticipated. The dance was crowded with the belles of Columbia and the officers of the Fort. I was happy to treat second lieutenants to the spectacle of their chaplain acting as aide to the general. We left before the dance was over and the general drove me back but had so much to talk about that we sat in his car in front of my quarters for half an hour. It was mostly a monologue: the general's.

Incidentally Mrs. T. is a nice widow of uncertain years. She has since showed some concern about entertaining me. Of course one hates to slight a widow especially as she has a mink coat already and you wouldn't have to buy her one. I think, however, I shall defer to my superior officers.

Tuesday and Wednesday I prepared a party for the mothers and children of the regiment. I filled Christmas boxes, the traditional Sunday school variety, with candy and nuts, and we had an orange in addition. I secured the names of the twenty-four children, the sex and age, and bought a gift for each. Then we concocted an entertainment with a soldier doing imitations of Donald Duck, and another playing the mouth organ, and a couple others singing songs. We all joined in carol singing. There was a Santa Claus and the distribution of gifts. I had arranged for two hundred soldiers to come to the party as spectators—to help fill the hall and to give them a taste of a children's Christmas. We picked men, as far as we could, who had children at home. They enjoyed it a lot.

Our big celebration was Christmas Eve. Since no hall was large enough to accommodate the regiment, we had fixed up the drill field with an outdoor stage at one end lit with floods. The field was ringed by trucks with their lights. A loudspeaker system was installed. There was a mammoth Christmas tree with hundreds of lights and a glittering star.

At seven-thirty the men were marched down to the field, three thousand of them. It was a balmy night, and quite clear. The long ranks coming into the field were an impressive sight—vague shapes in the darkness singing Christmas carols and songs like "Jingle Bells" as they marched toward us. From the stand I could hear them coming, company after company, and then see them as they swung into the light of the trucks and took their places in massed columns on the field. I found it very moving.

We had a fine program with talent, from a concert singer to a hillbilly. At the close the three thousand, led by a choir, joined in singing the Christmas carols and then marched off the field company by company, still singing. I could hear them as they separated to the various sections of the camp. I got a tremendous thrill.

There was a dance at the Service Club for enlisted men from 9:00 to midnight. Yet at 11:30 I had a candlelight carol service at the chapel. The service was simple with the singing of songs by the choir, the reading of the Christmas story, prayers for the folks back home, and the communion sacrament. We had a full house with ninety-eight receiving communion. Candles were the only light and the whole atmosphere was one of quietness and peace.

After our service was over I stayed up to pack some candy and nuts in boxes to take to the hospital on Christmas Day. We have ninety-eight patients there and I intended to see each one and bring him a remembrance from the regiment. I didn't get to bed very early, but I enjoyed assembling the gifts since this reminded me of fixing the plates of sweets at home the night before Christmas.

On Christmas Day, after a hurried breakfast, I hied me to my office. Alone in this comfortable room, I arranged all my Christmas gifts on a table and opened them at my leisure, with a thousand thronging thoughts of you and others who had remembered me. . . .

Our Christmas service had a fine attendance and I received many appreciative comments. We had a splendid dinner following, with all that is traditional. I spent the afternoon visiting the men at the hospital. . . .

Russell

On January 1, Stroup was formally appointed regimental chaplain to the 399th Infantry. As the next letter shows, he was happy to be the only Protestant on the team. Even in the army he remained an individualist who chafed at sharing responsibility.

Stroup joined the physical training of the regiment as much as his duties would permit: to become acquainted with the men, and to tone his thirty-seven-year-old body for the rigors of combat that he anticipated.

Wednesday, January 13, 1943

Dearest family,

. . . I am eager to get out in the field with the men again but have not felt that I should quite yet. Two battalions go each day to a training ground some three miles from here and stay all day. That would be a fine chance to be with the men without any interruptions. They started doing it when I was too busy to go, and now I've been unwell and couldn't, but I hope to start soon.

We have just received word that we are to get our third chaplain, who will arrive from Harvard the end of this month. He is to be a Jewish chaplain, assigned to our regiment but serving the Jews of the whole division. There will then be a Catholic, a Protestant, and a Jew with our group, which is good. I won't have to share the Protestant services with anyone. At least 50 percent of our men are from the eastern cities and consequently Catholic, and about 15 percent Jewish, and the rest nothing or Protestant. Just at the moment I have two Catholic men taking instruction to become Protestants—this, of course, at their insistence. . . .

Russell

The saved letters resume in April. By then, Stroup's commander wanted him with the troops at all times, even though this disrupted plans for a visit home.

Sunday, April 18, 1943

Dearest family,

By now you know why I am here and not with you after all my hopeful plans. Man proposes but the army, alas, disposes. I tried to persuade the colonel that we would not be necessary on his little expedition, but he couldn't see it that way. The funny thing was that the two other regiments would not allow their chaplains to go along, feeling that they would just be in the way; but ours doesn't feel that way about it, so off we went. . . .

Russell

The following humorous letter, undated, shows why the colonel might have wished to have Stroup accompany the troops on training maneuvers.

Dearest Mother & Cran, mostly Cran, I guess, in this letter—

Outside of the fact that I've had little sleep and almost no water, I'm in good shape. Just at the moment it's raining—the first we've had, and I think only a shower. I'm seeking the rather inadequate shelter of my pup tent and writing until the rain passes. The thunder and lighting make quite a display, with sound effects that might very well be part of our training program.

Tonight is, as they say, nontactical, which means we may have lights and a bonfire. I have planned an outdoor entertainment for the men which may be called off on account of the rain. It will be fairly simple, a good deal of group singing and some "artists" to perform—guitar players and "geetar" players, harmonica virtuosos, a lad on the accordion, and one with trumpet.

Last evening, Thursday, Chaplain Nuntory came over to say Mass, so once more I was detailed all the non-Catholics. I gave a talk to some four hundred men, which they received with great enthusiasm and, I hope, even some profit. We didn't try to have a service since singing was not allowed and, besides, I don't like to do it when the men are ordered to come. I did have a good talk for them which might have been called a sermon, prefaced by a good explanation of Protestant faith which precludes the possibility of compulsory religion. My theme was the necessity for discipline and, with this most unpopular subject, I think I succeeded in interesting and helping the men.

(One end of the pup tent is altogether open and that happens to be the end the rain is coming from so I'm crouched at the far corner but still not out of range.)

Wednesday night I went with a raiding party. Two of our toughest lieutenants were detailed to go on the mission, both of them with Ranger training, and I went along for fun and at their request. We were in fatigues with face and hands blackened—three men against a battalion that was waiting for what they thought would be a much larger attack. We got through the first outposts by stealth and found a tent with three men in it. These we awakened, wrapped bands over their mouths, and safely secured two. We compelled the third to go ahead of us, giving the password and leading us to the headquarters of the commanding officer.

We got right up to the guards of the C.O.'s tent when we were recognized and an alarm was sounded. The lieutenants threw the smoke bombs they were carrying, which would, theoretically, have blown up the headquarters, and we scattered into the darkness. The camp was awake by then with hundreds of men beating about looking for us. One of the lieutenants, not content with the smoke we had made, lit a fire and was discovered and captured. The other lieutenant escaped. So did I, creeping and crawling through "enemy" territory until I reached our lines. There I found the other lieutenant and we tried to get back through the lines again to find out what had happened, but they were all on the alert and it was difficult—mad too, since the lieutenants had not been very gentle with some of their men. We finally got back to camp rather late.

The next night, last night, we expected and received a return visit. To compensate for the damage we had done with three men, they came in force. But they received a warm reception and none penetrated our second lines. We captured almost sixty men during the evening and there was great excitement—also some rather rough-and-tumble encounters, with minor bruises, bumps, and a couple of bayonet cuts.

I was just wandering around to see what was going on and during the course of it ran into some of the "enemy" and was forced to capture a lieutenant and later a couple of privates. I didn't have any weapons, and was the chaplain, but these facts they didn't know until too late.

My main job, though, was to go from outpost to outpost encouraging our men; for many of them, alone and in the dark, were not a little nervous. I would help them feel safer and more on the alert. It was all lots of excitement for the men, and necessary training. It was very interesting to watch their reactions.

A lieutenant from the "enemy" attacked one of our sentries, but as bad luck would have it he happened to pick on Jiminez, who fought through the Spanish Civil War on the side of the loyalists. It was a rude encounter for the lieutenant. Only my fortunate arrival saved sad consequences.

(It's blowing a gale with hailstones big as mothballs falling around. I don't know whether the tent is going to stay with me or not. . . . It stayed, but there were anxious moments.)

I was on patrol with a sergeant, testing our own guards. With one we pretended not to know the password, and he started to drive us back to camp at bayonet point. He got too close, however, and the sergeant, with a quick move, disarmed him and then proceeded to lecture him on the proper procedure to employ. Apparently the lad learned his lesson, for some time later he came in with two real prisoners. . . .

Another problem last night was a night feeding—in the dark, without any lights. That is, of course, the way it would be done in combat: breakfast served before dawn, no lunch except emergency rations, and dinner brought up in trucks after dark. It all went off very well, but the men were plenty hungry when dinner finally arrived. So our days go by.

Given the choice of marching home tonight after midnight or Saturday morning early, our colonel chose Saturday, and so we pack up and leave here about 6:30 tomorrow, getting home before noon. One of the lieutenants is being married Saturday evening, with quite a party for him afterwards which I will attend for a while. Since I am one of the very few who could get into town this week, on both my trips in my jeep I have had to call up various young ladies—making dates for the officers. Just another of the chaplain's many and varied duties.

Well the rain has stopped and so must I. . . .

Russell

On April 23, Stroup received a promotion to the grade of captain.

Troop morale remained a problem. For Mother's Day—when young men might feel lonesome, or guilty of inattention—Stroup contrived an elaborate scheme to involve soldiers in honoring those mothers who lived on the base.

Monday, May 10, 1943

Dearest Mother and Cranston,

The day yesterday was a great success and worth the extensive work that I put in to make it so. Our fifteen mothers came out to the recreation hall, and assembled to greet them were six men from each company. I introduced the mothers to their respective company boys. The boys pinned corsages, which we had furnished, on their "mothers." After greetings on behalf of the regiment by the colonel, all proceeded to the chapel. Each mother sat in a pew with the six boys from "her" company. The pews were decorated at the ends with old-fashioned bouquets, the kind with little lace doilies on them, arranged by Private Schoutith. We had special music by the choir, and I gave a good sermon.

After service the ladies went to "their boys'" respective mess halls, where they sat at decorated tables with the luxury of table cloths. In most instances they were presented with another bouquet from the company. After dinner they were taken around the area and then sent home in taxis.

The boys had a grand time, and so did the mothers. They were profuse in their thanks and have been calling me all day to say so. It seems that the boys gave them a very good account of their chaplain and how much they thought of him. That pleased the ladies and pleases me. Today we are sending letters to the mothers of the boys who were in this service. I enclose a copy.

My dear Mrs.

As Chaplains of the regiment of which your son is a member, we feel you would be interested in knowing that although it was quite impossible for your son to be home with you on Mother's Day, he showed his respect for you by attending the Mother's Day Service held yesterday in the Regimental Chapel. . . .

To hope the joys of Mother's Day
May not be lessened in your heart
Because a loved one's far away,
But rather, may the day impart
A sense of pride no words can tell,
Abiding faith, a knowledge too,
That he will do his duty well
For God, for country, and for you.

Colonel Andrew C. Tychsen, Commanding Officer of this Regiment, joins us in sending greetings to you and our assurance that if in any way we may serve you or your son it will be our privilege to do so.

Sincerely,
Chaplains, 399th Infantry

We had a full house, so the job of getting the letters off is something. Everyone thought it was one of the most successful affairs that we have had. . . .

Every six months we have to give a sex morality lecture to the men of the regiment, and this is the week. For four days I speak to some eight hundred men a day on the subject. The colonel insists that I should be the one to do it and so the entire burden falls on me.

I had a long talk with the colonel on Saturday night about the morale of the regiment, which is not as good as it ought to be. I was quite frank and made some pointed suggestions to the colonel about what he should do. He has been trying to do what I suggested. I want him to get closer to the men—and in some way other than his usual role of critic. He has to criticize, and he has to discipline, but he should—as I told him—make a point to speak to the men on other occasions when he might praise. That he did at our meeting today. . . .

Russell

Friday, May 21, 1943

Dear Cran,

. . . Next week a couple of days I shall be out on the range, for there is to be carbine practice for those men who carry them and also attack under fire for all men. The goal is to advance under fire and capture what is called the Nazi village. You have to crawl through barbed wire entanglements and under machine-gun fire. I think my job will be to quiet the jittery nerves of some men who may be frightened.

Russell

Some of Stroup's older friends in Lynchburg remembered his account of this situation and passed it on to me: Infantrymen were required to crawl beneath a spray of live machine-gun fire, each cradling his rifle in his forearms. Some, in fear, refused to set forth, while others froze beneath the fire, hugging the ground. Stroup crawled out to these men, speaking words of encouragement, and accompanied the most fearful as they crept forward beneath the bullets.

In the days to come, Stroup's personal fitness program bore additional fruit.

Monday, May 24, 1943

Dearest family,

. . . I made the hike on Friday night as I told you and got through in good shape. That is, I made it, which is a lot more than many others did. We had a two-and-a-half-ton truck and two ambulances following the battalion, picking up men as they fell. Our third battalion did better than any other so far, but they still lost a lot of men. It was a grueling business—both the distance and the speed make it hard. You have to march fast, with short rest periods, to cover the twenty-five miles in eight hours—or seven and a half as we did, which was a record for the fort.

There were moments when I thought I might not make it, but I did. Of course, I haven't had the constant marching practice that the men have. I walked with the commander of K Company at the head of the column. We set the pace: that meant we had to keep going. When the march was over the company commander complimented the men on making it. He added, "And the chaplain was there all the time and came through with us," whereupon the men cheered. I have heard a lot about it since. I did what I wanted to do: made an impression and so helped the chaplains.

We rested most of Saturday. I was stiff and sore, but felt all right on Sunday. The 3d Battalion is a pretty rugged lot and the best marchers in the regiment. This is mostly a matter of morale, for on such a march you go the last ten miles on nerve and the will to do it. I like to think that their morale is due in part to the fact that they are the battalion I have worked with the most.

Well, I got through. Frankly, I don't quite know how I manage it at my age.

Russell

Monday, July 19, 1943

Dearest family,

. . . Did I tell you of the Jewish boy who came to see me recently to ask if I could help him not to hate the German people. He had escaped to this country, but his brother was gassed to death by the Germans in a concentration camp in Austria. His father is now in a concentration camp in Holland, where they fled first. When he last heard about his mother and sister, they were being shipped to Poland from Holland—to what fate it would be hard to imagine.

He wanted to know if he could be helped to keep from hating a people. For, he said, he grew up in Germany after the first World War and he knew how terrible hatred could be. He felt that the world could only be saved if hatred were eliminated and love took its place. This ought to shame some of our good Christian people who are hating for little cause: when a Jew who has reason, in the suffering of his race and of his family, can make such a plea. What a world we might make if we had more like him in it. . . .

Russell

[September, 1943]

Dearest family,

. . . On my report for this month the colonel put an endorsement as he always does, and the sergeant showed it to me because he thought it was so unusual. It ran something like this, "Chaplain Stroup continues to be an exemplary Regimental Chaplain doing work that is definitely superior. All are agreed on this."

Russell

Late in September, Stroup made a trip home to Virginia that occasioned another letter of commendation, this one from the chairman of the war bond campaign in Lynchburg.

September 28, 1943

The Commanding Officer
399th Infantry Regiment
Fort Jackson, S.C.
Dear Sir:

It is fitting for us to thank you for "loaning" Chaplain Russell Stroup to us for our bond promotion rally last Wednesday night. The plan of the rally was to sell bonds for tickets, and the sale amounted to $238,000. From the way the tickets sold the last day, your Chaplain and our friend helped a-plenty.

As usual he gave a talk that everyone had to apply to himself. Stroup has the ability, pleasantly, to drive home facts in such a way that one cannot misinterpret them. We miss him in Lynchburg. . . .

Chairman
War Finance Committee

At the end of October, Stroup received another commendation from his commanding officer, this one passed back to him from Memphis, Tennessee, by the supervising chaplain at 2d Army headquarters.

This Regiment leaves shortly for army maneuvers, and will not return to Fort Jackson. Our Chapel has been the most outstanding on the Fort, both for beauty and for attendance. Chaplain Stroup has been the guiding spirit and to him is due the credit for its unchallenged success. We leave behind us a beautiful Chapel, splendidly equipped as a legacy to the next unit occupying this area.

In mid-November, Stroup's regiment, the entire 100th Division, and at least one other division left for several months of maneuvers in the Cumberland hill country east of Nashville, Tennessee. In army jargon, they engaged in "problems"—battle situations. Stroup also dealt with other problems.

Dearest family,

We are out near Carthage, Tenn., but too far away from any large place to let the men get into town in large numbers. Since they were paid, I was afraid that all their money would go to the gamblers among us. Consequently, I arranged to get money order blanks. We chaplains, with our assistants, set up in the post office business and took the boys' money. We will exchange it for money orders on Monday when I get into town.

Right now I am much concerned that I have on my person over five thousand dollars in cash for which I am responsible. I had no idea that the response would be so great. That five thousand is saved from the clutches of the men who prey on the weaknesses and the boredom of their victims to get their hard-earned money from them.

Chaplain Brown took his job very seriously and went around from crap game to crap game urging the men to put their money into money orders. However, the record was from the 3d Battalion, which I managed. . . .

Russell

[after Thanksgiving 1943]

Dearest Mother and Cranston,

Our first "problem" went off very well. I was neither killed, captured, wounded, nor too uncomfortable. The weather was favorable, not too cold, and early in the problem the two divisions reached a stalemate, which meant that we didn't move around very much.

My part in this was not very glorious except in one instance where I served to secure information from "prisoners of war." Our intelligence officers and special interrogating officers, with a fine disregard for human psychology, had failed. So I took it up and, using just the old friendly approach, soon had them talking freely and spilling all the information that the division critically needed. Our regiment was particularly commended for getting this information—but, of course, outside of the regiment the credit went to the intelligence service and not to the chaplain. I wonder if they will ever learn how to approach and handle men. I doubt it. . . .

At the critique, they said that our first "problem" had been conducted better than any other in Tennessee maneuvers. It was also stated that our men behaved themselves much better in towns and in Nashville than any other troops. I have noted that myself; it is a repetition of our experience in Columbia. Considering the generally poor background of our men, I think that the chaplains deserve a lot of the credit for this behavior. It is gratifying to go to town and see, among all the rowdy and drunken soldiers, our own men looking and behaving so well. And they are always glad to run into the chaplain wherever they are.

Our regiment continues to have the best reputation within our division. The Red Cross man was commenting recently that we had fewer welfare cases than any other regiment. Comparatively few men from our regiment go to the Red Cross for help. Of course that is because, in our regiment, they see the chaplain first. . . .

I was glad that there was so much for me to do on Thursday that I had little chance to remember the Thanksgivings of the past, and the one I was missing at home. . . .

I wish you could see the camp we have here that Emile [Stroup's assistant] has set up: the two pup tents side by side, surrounded by ditches to take off rainwater; the jeep and trailer behind the tents (we have a jeep and driver assigned to us now); field desk set up under a tree in front of the tents; a fire burning nearby; and over it all the chaplain's flag flying to remind men where we are, and to bring them to us. It is quite complete. How thankful I continue to be for my sleeping bag and rubber mattress. I am the only man who sleeps in pajamas, but I would be too warm in the bag with my clothes on, and much more uncomfortable.

Russell

Hotel Hermitage, Nashville, Tenn.
[early December 1943]

Dearest family,

The third "problem" ended at twelve noon today, and a half hour afterwards I was on my way out of the woods to Nashville, eager to get a shower, clean sheets, and a good night's rest—also a real meal on a table with a linen cloth. I have now had all that, except the sleep, and I will get that when I finish this letter.

Last night there wasn't much sleep for me. Late in the afternoon I had to inform one of our men of the death of his mother, secure him a furlough, and rush him to the train at Lebanon. This meant driving through our lines and the "enemy" lines with no special privileges for a chaplain—immanent danger of capture and delay. It was a nasty, rainy night—in our favor—and by clever driving and a lot of bluffing I drove forty miles one way and forty-five returning without capture. I got the boy off.

I found that if you put on your headlights and drive boldly without any attempt at concealment, you give puzzled sentries a feeling that whether they understood it or not you must have some authority for doing something so contrary to all rules and custom. During the trip I observed that a big offensive against us was beginning but, of course, I would not divulge anything discovered on such an errand. Yet I was eager to get back to our outfit.

We were holding the flank and, after a night of driving rain that soaked everything, we were awakened out of damp and fitful slumber by the sound of firing. We found that the 14th Armored Division had been thrown against us in force. Tanks and half-tracks were milling all over the place in the half-light of a rainy dawn. Fortunately, although we were surprised we were not panicked. We succeeded in the almost incredible task of holding off the division with our one regiment. As a soldier from the 14th Armored told me on the street in Nashville tonight, "You sure gave us one hell of a fight!"

We did have the advantage of hilly terrain unsuited to tanks, and a day and night of rain that made fields and roads quagmires of mud. Thousands of vehicles (or so it seemed) struggled on the narrow roads. One of my self-imposed tasks was to try to straighten out tangled traffic. It was quite a morning and I was a very dirty boy when I got into Lebanon to change my clothes for Nashville. . . .

Russell

The 100th Division would continue maneuvers into January and eventually be shipped to Europe. However, soon after his Nashville leave, Stroup received orders removing him from the regiment that he had come to know so well and intended to accompany into battle.

After receiving a phone call from Stroup, his mother added a note to the letter above before forwarding it to her sister in California: "This came yesterday morning just before Russell learned he was having to leave his men and go to another outfit. You can see by this letter what it will mean to him. I am so sorry about it, and so sorry for him."

2

"This Outfit Is Hot"

Hotel King, Tullohoma, Tenn.,
Friday, December 14, 1943

Dearest family,

. . . I arrived here on Tuesday afternoon to find that this outfit is, as they say, "hot." They are planning to move out by next Tuesday, and most of the men are packed and ready to go. Where we are going and what our address will be I don't know. The rumor is that they are going West to California. . . . Of course it would be a disappointment to me to go to the Pacific but I must feel, as I do, that all my ways are ordered not by the War Department but by God, and trust in His will. . . .

Fortunately the outfit is a good one with fine young men in it from the Middle West, etc., mostly Protestants. There are only about a thousand altogether and I have a Catholic chaplain under me. The chaplain who preceded me was an older man from the last war, too old to go across. . . .

There are a thousand thoughts thronging my mind and it is hard to write. You know I love you both so much. My one regret is that my movements may cause you apprehension or anxiety or sorrow. Please try not to let them. We have known this would be, or might be. All I have done has been done in prayer, and all will be well, I know. I shall certainly (and I mean this) take care, very good care, of myself—and the Heavenly Father will care for me, too. You both take care of yourselves, and we shall all be together again before long. Darlings, I love you—

Russell

The "outfit" was the 1112th Engineer Combat Group, about to start its journey to the South Pacific. This was a special unit of the U.S. Army Corps of Engineers, equipped and trained to land just behind a first wave of invading troops in order to construct docking facilities, build roads, and rehabilitate bombed Japanese airfields for American use. The men tended to be older and better educated than those in an infantry unit. Immediately upon his arrival, Stroup was appointed group chaplain.

When Stroup was able to phone his home, he learned that Cranston had been hospitalized. His mother, now at home alone, was anxious that both her sons seemed to be moving away from her, into greater danger.

[Sunday, December 16, 1943]

Dearest Mother and Cranston,

I must express my very deep concern over the condition in which I seem to have put you both. It is hard to think of Cranston in the hospital, even if just for a checkup, and of Mother left alone at home. I feel extremely guilty. Having gone into the army because I could not bear the thought of millions of men suffering, without sharing that with them, I find that the suffering I endure is nothing compared to the suffering I cause the innocent members of my family. It is foolish to think of this now, as it can't be helped, but I do hope with all my heart that you will both keep as well as possible. It would be a sad thing for me—after imagining through these months the joys of coming home—to have no one to come home to. . . .

I have already had more stimulating conversations with the officers here than I had in all my experience with the 399th. These are, without exception, college men, as are many of the privates and noncoms. In this outfit every one of the majors is a graduate from some outstanding university: Carnegie Tech, Massachusetts Institute of Technology, Texas A&M, V.P.I., California, etc. . . .

As far as the chaplain's work is concerned there is much to be done. They had an old army chaplain, one only, with them for a long time. He just retired. He had done nothing but hold down his job and wait. Everyone liked him, but no one paid him any attention. They used his typewriters, field desks, and so forth, and he made no objection. He had no place for services. The result is that I have to start from scratch. There are lots of things to do, but they will be done.

I had just a handful out for worship this morning, but this handful included our colonel who, I am told, had never appeared before. . . .

Just this moment, I saw the orders for our departure—to San Francisco.

Russell

It is possible that I may patiently wait for my own funeral service but short of that I am a restless soul who cannot abide inaction and when it becomes not a matter of hours but of days the itch to be off is terrific. With Shakespeare I would say, "if it's to be done, let it be done quickly." The two hours I sat waiting for a call to go through to Lynchburg only filled a small part of the day.

It was in fact interesting to sit there and listen to one man after another talking—for the last time in a long time—to the folks at home. You could sense the courage at the other end; the studied nonchalance at both ends; the soldier's effort to give assurance that all was well with him; and his apparent concern for how the loved ones at home would be taking it. Of course they took it well because they made themselves, which didn't fool him, for he knew they were making this effort on his behalf.

My room, which was heaped with baggage, is empty now. We are allowed to take three things other than what we carry on our persons: a footlocker (trunk), a piece of hand luggage, and a bedding roll. The three together must not weigh more than 175 pounds. You try to fill them with what must last you six months at an unknown destination. We who have our wants stimulated for years, until we feel that every luxury is a necessity, must now cut to the bone.

Perhaps the lesson may be a good one and, like Thoreau, we will learn how little of material things are really necessary for life. But I fear that the opposite will be true and that millions of men, deprived for the duration of the things they so much want, will engage in a veritable orgy of accumulation when they get home. For myself, I feel a strange contradiction. You know how I love things and what pleasure I get in their possession, feeling they are mine. And yet whenever I go through such a process of elimination I experience relief that burdens have been taken away. I feel freer for divesting myself of this and of that.

This probably reveals my character. If I were a conservative I would not feel such relief. However, being interested in every new thing and desirous of it, I am a radical, of a sort. . . .

I haven't the slightest feeling of apprehension. This surprises me. I have never felt more calm or confident, even though on other occasions I have become quite apprehensive about things. A lot of men here, most of them, can imagine many things happening to them. I can't imagine anything harmful happening to me. That may be my supreme egoism, or it may be my faith—I don't know. I feel as sure that all will be well with me as I am that the sun will rise tomorrow. I think this is due in part to the fact that I know I have had good training—better training than even these men—in the line of caring for oneself in combat. As for the voyage, I look forward to it. . . .

Russell

When Stroup was in high school and college, he enjoyed train trips nearly every summer between California and Cleveland—in the company of his mother and his brother and sister.

[On the train West]

It would be very "right" if every group going overseas could cross the continent as we have done—could see America, even fleeting glimpses from a flying train. They would leave America with a more definite and reasonable pride in the nation which they serve and of which they are a part. . . .

This is a deluxe way of going to war—the most comfortable sort of living I have had since coming into the army. On the train are a number of cars of the old tourist type that we used to ride to California. The enlisted men are in these, three to each section, two occupying a lower berth and one the upper berth. In the compartment or drawing room at the end of the car, where we used to travel as a family, the noncommissioned officers live. At the end of the train there are standard Pullmans for the officers. Each car has a porter, and berths are made up just as on a civilian train. Two baggage cars have been converted to kitchens where food is prepared and taken through the cars to the men. . . .

Christmas Eve found everyone just a bit down in spirits. Most of the men didn't have many gifts, as their mail was somewhere en route. The game set that you sent me is quite the nicest around, already much admired and used by all. I played the first game on it, but since then it has become common property. So far chess has been the game, but others will be tried later.

To brighten Christmas Eve the officers made a chorus and went through the train singing Christmas carols in each coach. This was much appreciated by the men. They were in bed but not asleep, so the old familiar music was a benediction to the day.

Christmas morning it was snowing and the ground was covered. About ten o'clock the sun came out. At ten-thirty we stopped the train for a Christmas service that was held in a field by the tracks, not far from a little Utah town. For thirty minutes we sang carols: "O Come All Ye Faithful," "It Came upon a Midnight Clear," "Hark, the Herald Angels Sing," "O Little Town of Bethlehem," "Silent Night," and "Joy to the World." I read the Christmas story, gave a little talk, and led in prayer. I told them of the first Christmas and the little family that was far from home in a strange place with no shelter but a stable, yet the light of God was over the place, and there was a star in the night, and promise in an angel's song. I spoke of sacrifice—ours, that we might achieve a world safe for Christmas.

Back on board the train we had our Christmas meal: turkey, dressing, mashed potatoes, string beans, celery, fruit cup, pumpkin pie, and coffee with candy and nuts, etc. It was quite a feast.

Russell

Tuesday, December 28, 1943
"Somewhere on the west coast"

Dearest family,

One of the first things brought to our attention here is the matter of censorship. We are given complete instructions on the subject. Most of the rules are what one's common sense might suggest, but some are peculiar rules that must have some explanation—what it is I cannot imagine. We are not permitted to suggest where we are other than to say we are "somewhere on the west coast," but it is all right for me to say that Wednesday I shall go in to San Francisco to take care of business in connection with my work. I'm looking forward to that since it has been a long time between visits. . . .

Russell

While Russell, his brother, and his sister were attending Stanford University during the 1920s, they visited San Francisco frequently. Cranston, a poet, was part of a community there of writers, artists, and musicians. However, because the Stroups had moved east in 1934, they had not seen the great bridges built later that decade.

Friday, December 31, 1943

Dearest family,

I have been to San Francisco. It is quite the nicest thing that has happened. Everything was just as always, even the fog and the rain. There are changes, of course, but San Francisco is a woman who changes and yet remains her fascinating self. The most noteworthy additions are the bridges. I crossed the Bay Bridge and saw the Golden Gate Bridge. I had feared they might take something from the bay, but they don't.

I kept wishing all the time that Cranston were here. I know how much he would love it. All over town there are memories.

Tonight is New Year's Eve without any particular plans for a celebration. I certainly will be up when our New Year comes in, at least. We have little to regret in the passing of 1943 but may look forward with faith and hope to a 1944 that will bring to the world, and to us, the joy of Peace and the beginning, we pray, of a better day.

Loads of love,

Russell

Saturday, January 1, 1944
[then Monday, January 3]

I got your telegram today, and it rejoiced my heart to know that Cranston is doing so much better. . . .

It is still raining, which rather depresses the spirits. A little sunshine would have a tonic effect on us all. We have a right to expect a bit in California. The Chamber of Commerce ain't what it used to be.

Tomorrow is Sunday, but I don't anticipate it. The outfit just hasn't known what it is to have a chaplain who really did something, and apparently they never got into the habit of going to church. It will take some time to develop that. I resent a service with only a handful present—not that I mind the handful, but it infuriates me to think that some duck sat here on the job for months and when he left had no more to show for it. In fact it would have been better if they had no chaplain, for then the novelty of one might tempt some out. As it is they have become quite immune to the influence. I feared this might happen to me, and it has.

I'll have to begin all over to build something up. The trouble is that the best entrée I had in the old outfit was my participation in all the work of the men. With these men the training period is over, so that isn't possible. It is ironic that I should put forth so much effort to gain the trust, confidence, and affection of men and then not be able to profit from that in combat conditions. In my report this month I went to some pains to inform the chief of chaplains what I think of this kind of business. . . .

This is Monday. Much to my surprise there was a fine attendance at church service—about three times as many as they have ever had before. I think this was due to the fact that we are anticipating a journey but, whatever the cause, we had a fine service and I am gratified.

Russell

The Engineer Group departed for the Pacific Theater on January 5, 1944. Eastern New Guinea, toward which Stroup now headed, had been a colony of Australia, while the western half had been a Dutch colony until the Japanese invasion. It was not until June that Stroup, writing from New Guinea, could give details of the ocean voyage.

I am allowed to tell you now that we came over from the states on the Dutch ship *Kota Agoong*, chartered from the Dutch government by the U.S. It was not as nice as traveling on an American boat but interesting in that I got a chance to meet a lot of Dutchmen and their Javanese and Malay crew. The ship had cruised about the Netherlands East Indies before the war, carrying freight and a few passengers.

I don't know where you figured I was when I first got over here, but now I am allowed to say that we landed at Goodenough Island, which you can perhaps find on a large map. It is in the D'Entrecasteaux Group of Islands off the coast of New Guinea. Since we got there shortly after the island had been taken there was not much excitement. Once in a while someone rounded up a Jap and there were, in the first couple of weeks, a few light air raids, but that was all. . . . I was supposedly in the combat zone, but that is an elastic term.

Goodenough Island had been invaded by U.S. forces in August and September 1943. After two years of reverses at the hands of the Japanese, American forces in the Pacific were just beginning to take the offensive. Stroup's unit arrived there the following February, months after most Japanese had withdrawn, and remained until April. During this time Goodenough Island served as a staging area for troops preparing for a major invasion further to the west.

In the first letter written after his arrival there that has been saved, we find Stroup, bored by inactivity, dreaming of ways to reform the American Protestant churches he had left behind.

Tuesday, March 28, 1944

Dearest family,

. . . My status is unchanged. I am doing what work I can in the one battalion but have considerable time on my hands. I'm using the time to outline a book on the Church. The title, "A Lover's Quarrel," suggests the purpose of the book. I took it from Robert Frost, "I have a lover's quarrel with the world." I want to write constructive criticism, but with no holds barred. I imagine these chapter headings: Dove-Like Divines, Gnat Strainers, The Walking Dead, Poison and Pap, The Clank of Coins, The Ministry of Fear, Tilting at Windmills, The Assembly of the Lukewarm, The Gospel Gestapo, A Horse and Buggy Church, There Ought to Be a Law, The Sons of Martha, The Vanishing Protestant, Uniformity or Unity, Our Lost Simplicity, etc.

I have a certain critical faculty that should be utilized for some good purpose. I chose to begin this rather than a book on war because it provides me some escape from the things that so intimately concern me here. I started out writing an article—but every paragraph seemed to want to become a chapter.

Russell

Little came of this study, for in less than a month Stroup would choose to focus his writing on the scenes of war before him.

He mailed his next letter in the hope that it might reach Emma by April 30, her sixty-eighth birthday. As a young woman, Emma had for several years traveled across Ohio preaching as a popular Methodist evangelist.

Monday, April 10, 1944

Dearest Mother,

Soon you will have a birthday—soon considering the distance this letter must travel to bring my gift of love to you on that day. . . .

The supreme sacrifice I make in the army is the loss of years with you. I hate the thought of that. Every day I am conscious of the moments that I miss, and with all my heart I wish that it were otherwise. I feel ashamed that I have left you with added burdens rather than being with you to help bear the ones you have. And yet I know that I am here because of you: there was something you gave to me that made it impossible to "pass by on the other side" when men are suffering the torment of war. I had to be faithful to the example you gave me of sacrificial service for others, at whatever cost to self.

Recently I have been receiving replies to letters I sent to the mothers of the men whom I have led to the Lord. Perhaps the best birthday gift that I can give to you is this knowledge of the joy in their hearts for the salvation of their boys. You have made this possible by your

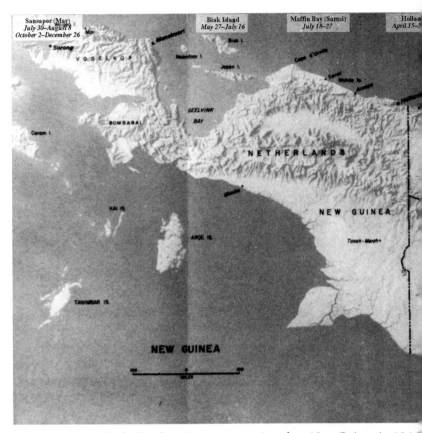

The locations at which Chaplain Stroup was stationed on New Guinea in 1944.
From Robert Ross Smith, Approach to the Philippines, *map II.*

dedication of me to the service of Christ. I know that the deepest satisfaction in your own life came from bringing men and women into the saving knowledge of the Son of God. Your ministry has never ceased, and now it is increased by one who is proud to minister in your name.

Your loving son,

Russell

At the top of the letter Emma wrote, "Received May 1, 1944," the day after her birthday. Well before that date, Stroup's time of impatient waiting had ended. He dated his next letter April 18, but it was probably written on

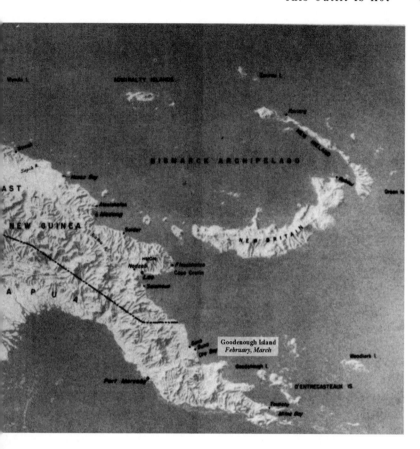

Goodenough Island
February, March

Saturday the fifteenth, or before, for he boarded ship on the morning of the eighteenth. He confused, as well, the date of the Sunday letter that followed.

Dearest Mother and Cranston and Margretta,
 . . . The other night I went out riding with one of the officers in his jeep and we got stuck in the mud. We called up the camp and they brought a four-ton wrecker to pull us out. It did, but then got stuck itself. We drove the jeep toward help for the wrecker, but got it stuck again. Then we walked into camp and returned in a four-ton truck. It was unable to budge the wrecker, although it did get our jeep out. We

then fetched a six-ton truck, which is plenty large, but it with the four-ton managed to accomplish nothing, except getting stuck themselves. Then we sent for a D8 Bulldozer—which Cranston knows is really something!—but that got stuck too.

Not until the next day did we manage to get all of them out. This gives you some idea of what mud is like here. We had about a hundred thousand dollars worth of equipment bogged down in an effort to extricate one jeep.

To write is difficult, not because there is nothing to tell, but because at the moment I can't tell it.

Russell

Sunday [April 16, 1944]

Dearest Mother,

. . . Had a good Sunday today. Preached to a full house at the Chapel. My text was from the first chapter of Joshua, "Be strong and of good courage; be not afraid, neither be thou dismayed: for the LORD thy God is with thee whithersoever thou goest." It made an effective and timely message. We closed with the stirring words of the hymn I like so much, "Lead On, O King Eternal."

Russell

On Monday morning, just before his ship loaded, Stroup dashed off a note to be mailed from Goodenough Island. He attempted to reassure his family— quite erroneously, as it turned out—that his role with the engineering unit would shield him from danger.

Monday, April 17, 1944

Dearest family,

Monday is usually a day when I would recover from Sunday. Unfortunately, there is too much to do this particular Monday to allow time for recuperation.

. . . I probably will see combat. You will want to know, for your comfort, just what this will mean for me. All operations out here are landing ones. The original landing force moves in and takes over the beach, etc. After the infantry and artillery have established themselves with the help of amphibian engineers (which we are not), then we move in. So naturally all the real fighting is over by the time we get there. All we have to face is the possibility of bombing; perhaps artillery

David Segel, a soldier on Goodenough Island, painted for Stroup a watercolor of the handsome thatched chapel where troops gathered for worship under his leadership.

fire, though not likely; and possibly raiding parties of Japs. It is not very hazardous and nothing to worry you.

Of all groups that really see action, ours will be in the safest position.

I shall go ashore with my jeep and trailer. For Cranston's sake I might point out that I could take with me all the weapons I might want—from a carbine to a tommy gun—as there are plenty available. There is usually one of the latter in each vehicle. But you know me. It isn't only the rules regarding chaplains, but also my own inclination, that will keep me unarmed.

The more I share with the men out here, the more I know that my conscience could not rest if they were taking punishment while I was safe and comfortable back home.

However, if I earn a medal it will only be for the mental anguish of being away from you who are so dear to me. I'll dispense with the medal if I can return to you both.

Russell

3

"What Am I Doing Here?"

[first day on the convoy, Monday, April 17, 1944]

Dearest family,

The good-byes were said this morning. "Good luck." "Thanks." "I'll be seeing you." "Sure." "Take care of yourself." "You know me." And we are gone. The jeep bounces down the familiar roads. Off to the right against the hill is a chapel where I held services—over there is a deserted campsite, which was home for a month—here I saw a movie—there I visited the casualties. As we pass the airstrip I glimpse the slouchy Aussies, good fellows, tough but pleasant. We drive past the dock where we landed after a long, long voyage. It seems years ago. As the army intended, the weeks here have made me feel like a veteran, which, of course, I am not. The long line of docks is now crowded with transports. The shore is lined with LSTs [landing ship, tank]. Out in the harbor are more ships. Planes drone overhead. All is bustle, lines of men, piles of equipment.

We reach our own LST, its great gaping mouth ready to swallow us like so many Jonahs—indeed hardly noticing our little selves having already digested such a meal of trucks, tanks, bulldozers, steam shovels, and the incredible amount of gear belonging to an outfit such as ours. The vehicles are waterproofed against the surf on some strange beach that is our destination. Their wheels are turned in the direction they must go. They will come off in a rush.

I climb to the upper deck and make my way aft to cabins for the officers. Everything is clean and orderly—"shipshape." We gawk at the unfamiliar sight of electric lights, bunks, and chairs. I feel the mattress and springs on the bed. How long since I slept in such luxury! In the "head" are porcelain basins. I take a childish delight in washing with hot water. In the little dining salon colored men are setting the table with china and silver. Of course, such elegance is reserved for officers. The men bunk between decks, or in the vehicles topside. . . .

Only the sailors, and our administrative officers, are busy. The rest of us have nothing to do. Standing by the rail to watch the sea is enough for me. I also have a couple of books I hope to read. Some officers have started the inevitable poker game that will last as long as the voyage.

The ship pulls away from shore, pointing her prow toward the unknown. I know I cannot drift beyond His love and care.

The convoy included 113 transport ships, nearly half of which were LSTs. Fourteen of these were escort destroyers that also carried troops for the landing. This was the largest operation yet undertaken in the Southwest Pacific area.

After boarding the ship, Stroup focused his writing on the experience at hand. He composed essays daily, to be mailed home upon landing. Later, in combat, he wrote a long, descriptive letter each day that it was possible to do so. The shipboard essays were written by hand, for Stroup's typewriter was stored with other gear.

Cranston was so impressed by the literary quality of these essays that he carefully transcribed a dozen, from shipboard and from subsequent combat, in a double-spaced typescript with several carbon copies, intending to solicit a publisher. Stroup, as we shall see, counseled against immediate publication on the grounds that this might violate army regulations. Although he hoped to edit this material for publication after his return home, he did not want letters written under stress to become public without his prior review. However, from time to time he also sent home articles intended for publication, which he encouraged Cranston to market on his behalf.

[second day]

Dearest family,

It takes all kinds of men to make a world, or to make a war, and we have them. The skipper is from Falmouth town where men have gone down to the sea in ships for two hundred years. His leathery face looks like the sea; it can be placid or stormy. He is all business. He reads orders for the expedition as though they were directions for a cruise. He came from the North Atlantic patrol, the hardest theater of a hard war. In the Southwest Pacific he has driven his ship onto some of the bloodiest beaches of the war, put men and equipment ashore and gotten off again. He knows what we will face. Under his calm recital of the details of attack I feel his sympathy for what we may go through. "I think, Padre, it might be a good idea to have a service for the men the night before we land."

Later I remarked, "In all the instructions you read to us, nothing is said about what should be done if the initial attack fails." "We go ahead according to schedule." I think we will. I don't think we shall fail. If we pull this off it will mean a new phase in the war out here. I'm glad I'm riding with a Falmouth man.

There is an officer from the Marines with the nose of a pugilist, the chin of a man who presses forward, and the clear eyes of a small boy. He looks older than he is: he was at Guadalcanal. His admiration for his men is boundless. "I saw those kids fight for days and weeks in swamps, raining day and night, some with their feet rotting off in the wet and mud." He watches, with silent concern, our young innocents who talk so gaily of their keenness for combat. "I've been out here two years," he says. "I reckon I could do with a little of home."

There is a young Javanese officer, so tiny, seemingly so delicate, with the dark liquid eyes of a deer. He speaks excellent English. "We, in Java, are a nation with an old, old civilization. We are inferior to no people, save that we never learned to fight. This is a world where those who love peace have no place."

We came away from our late home loaded with extras. I have seen two parrots, a dog, and a cat, and more may turn up.

Stroup, himself, was one of the extras on this voyage. Despite the assurances he gave to his family, he had taken temporary leave from the 1112th Engineer Group in order to travel with the 239th Combat Engineer Battalion, which was entering combat for the first time.

Just before we sailed a jeep rushed down to the ship. Two men piled out and came running over to me. "Gee, Chaplain," one said, grabbing my hand, "I was afraid we'd miss seeing you to say good-bye." They were from the Group, and I assured them that I would be back with them, since the colonel had received a promise from the corps chaplain that I would be returned to the Group when this operation is over. I am only loaned, not transferred. On the other hand, the men of the battalion are delighted to find that I am here, for there was a question right up to the last minute whether I would get my orders to come along. I'm happy to be here, for I should have hated to have these men go out in this big show, leaving me behind just when I might be of value to them.

The portion of the battalion on this LST is almost 85 percent Protestant and at least 75 percent from the South. If you're going to be where there's fighting, they are comforting boys to have along. As one lad from the hills put it, "I cain't say as how I kere a heap fur fightin' but I reckon that's what we come here fur, and I aims to do my share."

[third day]

Dearest family,

. . . You think, "What's it going to be like?" You wonder, "How am I going to take it?" I think that few men fear that they will be killed. Somehow the mind hesitates to contemplate the possibility of one's own destruction. I think the men do imagine the possibility of wounds, but seldom death. . . .

Have I described our remarkable jungle hammocks that are waterproof, mosquito-proof, and not too uncomfortable? I want one when the war is over—perfect for camping out. Our jungle packs are also ingenious devices to hold an awful lot, everything in waterproof bags. Our uniforms are, of course, fatigues, and most of them are camouflaged. Each man has a knife and a machete. Fatigues serve for pajamas as well as day wear because, of course, you must be ready at all times to climb out of your hammock and into a foxhole. We all carry emergency rations in case we are unable to get fancy food right away.

If I had to be in action, I am fortunate to get into something as important as this assault. It will give me a second campaign star and, if I do my job, add a couple of stars to my heavenly crown. Of course it's possible that about the time we land they'll start invading France and crowd our news right off the front page. You'll only be able to read about us by searching through the ads.

Russell

[fourth day]

Dearest family,

We plod through the broad expanse of water toward our goal. The convoy moves like a herd of cows, while on the flanks the watchful destroyers linger like cowboys slouching in their saddles, seemingly unmovable—but every now and then putting spurs to their horses to canter to a new position guiding the deliberate herd. We rejoice in an overcast sky and drizzling rain because it lowers visibility and minimizes the risk from Japanese planes. They are a constant threat not only because of the damage they might do but because of what they might learn of our movements.

The men shower in the rain, stripping themselves on deck to wash off dust and grime. Many do laundry here as well, a never-ending task.

Nights are hot, shut behind closed doors and portholes. It is hard to woo reluctant slumber. I turn and toss and sweat and sweat until, at long last, fitful sleep comes. I dream strange dreams, always of home. . . .

Russell

[fifth day]

Dearest Mother and Cranston,

Last evening was blessed with one of those incredibly glorious sunsets that leave you uplifted. Our only tribute could be reverent silence. The men lined the rail looking in wonder toward the west. No sound save the rumble of engines broke the stillness. The setting sun had spread a crimson carpet across the water from our ships to a distant island, dark blue against the horizon, while above it the clouds were massed in ascending tiers toward heaven. For almost an hour, a changing pattern of flaming color made it seem as though the glory of the celestial was reflected in the clouds. I think we all felt that the heavens were "declaring the glory of God," and we had caught a vision of His presence.

I watched to the end and beyond, as the color faded like the echo of great music, and the sky and sea were dark and still, and the first stars came out. I prayed earnestly for these boys of mine, and those other boys, ahead of us, who so soon will be in the fury of combat. The whole tragedy of a mad world seemed accentuated by the peace of God all about me. The thought of this, and of the future, kept me awake for hours.

Here, surrounded by beauty and peace, we proceed fearfully on our mission of destruction. We are both hunting and hunted. Our mission mocks the moment of peace we felt. The vision was ephemeral, for a submarine might emerge from the crimson glory of the sea, a surface raider might appear from behind the magic isle, or destroying planes could sweep from the open heavens.

All over the world, millions of men share this paradox. We are just a small part.

I have asked myself so many times, "What am I doing here?" It isn't easy to answer. I love peace so passionately and hate war so utterly. More than a hatred: I am convinced that war is utterly futile and senseless. I see no good in it, nor any health coming from it, and yet here I am in the midst of it, feeling that it is right for me to be here and that, indeed, I could be nowhere else—even though this might cost me my life, with all that might mean in heartache and hardship for others. When I try to analyze the reasons I feel this way, it is hard.

There is the challenge of the work. Here are men who need me. One might have a similar ministry at home, yet nowhere else could one meet, on such intimate terms, so many men in so receptive a frame of mind. I feel that the church has never faced a greater opportunity: a heaven-sent chance to touch tomorrow's manhood and to save America for Christ. . . .

I look beyond the present to the future. I may be mistaken, but I doubt that there can be effective leadership in the church of tomorrow by men who, able to serve in the war, chose not to do so. Too many of our church men will be veterans. Too many of our families will have been affected. . . .

It will be similar for the Peace movement. When I was active, before, in this movement, I appreciated this lack: I could not speak as one having authority for I had never "been there" myself. Now I will be able to speak. Since Peace is the cause, above all others, to which I have dedicated myself, any sacrifice is worthwhile to render my efforts more effectual, if I am spared to carry them on.

I have also felt that, as part of a generation that failed to prevent this war, I should suffer with those who are the victims of our failure. Surely the young boys out here are less guilty than we. I must follow the Master: He would be found where mankind is suffering, and He would be sharing that suffering.

There is also the motive of "patriotism." I have always loved America deeply. I love the land, the people, the history, the ideals that make our country. Being an American, I have received so much for which I never paid, but which was bought for me at a price by the men and women of the past. There is a debt of love I owe. I cannot be indifferent to the call of my country, even though I may hate what we are called upon to do. . . .

We are compelled to halt the aggression of an evil movement in the world. I do not think war will make a better world. In many ways the world will be in a worse plight because of it. But if we had stood by and allowed the Nazi, the Fascist, and the militarist to run wild in our world, the darkness would become deeper and the night longer. . . .

I dread the thought of living in a world devastated spiritually and physically by war, but I dread more the thought of living in a world dominated by corrupt men who glorify all that I think of as evil and attack all that I conceive to be good. It is absolutely essential that we should fight against these evil forces. I wish with all my heart that we had perfected some nonviolent means of doing so, but we have not, nor could we now develop them in time. . . .

Ever since I was a little fellow, I have hated a bully. To stand by and see nations ride roughshod over weaker nations—I would forfeit my own self-respect.

This is an age of revolutionary strife. We are forced to take sides within our own nation and between nations. I want to be found on the side of the dignity and worth of human personality, of liberty, of the rights of man. I want to be found opposing tyranny, oppression, bigotry, and the exultation of materialism. I do not think that God blesses war, but I do hope that He blesses those who, in good conscience, are willing to sacrifice, in peace or war, for what they believe are principles in accord with His Holy Will. . . .

With understanding and without hate, I shall see the thing through to a victory that will be the beginning of the real task. When victory comes, I hope to go forward with the creative work of Peace, better prepared to play my part because of what I have been through.

Pray for me that I do not fail my men or myself, or the cause to which I have always dedicated myself. I hope that what I do now will justify the sacrifice I have forced you, as well, to make.

Love,

Russell

Stroup took the advice of the "skipper from Falmouth" and arranged a full day of religious services immediately prior to landing. He wrote of the day as "Sunday," but in fact it was Saturday, for Stroup's LST would land on the beach at Hollandia, on the north coast of New Guinea in what had been the Dutch half of the island, early Sunday morning.

Dear Ones,

Sunday has almost gone, leaving behind a feeling of satisfaction and thankfulness for a day blessed by consciousness that God has been here. I had two services—both were good! At ten o'clock we all gathered on the forward deck, under the sky with the sea all around us, and worshiped God. The sailors were particularly thankful for the service since it had been a long time since most of them had the opportunity. I talked from John 3:16 ["For God so loved the world, that he gave his only begotten Son, that whosoever believeth in him should not perish, but have everlasting life."] I stressed the fact that in a world of hate there is a God of Love, in a world of greed there is a God who Gave, in a world of bigotry there is a God whose salvation extends to "whosoever believeth," in a world of skepticism there is a God who calls us to believe, and in a world where death is everywhere there is a God who gives us eternal life through Christ.

In the evening, just as the sun was setting, we celebrated Holy Communion—again on the deck—and a goodly number of men knelt to receive the sacred elements in remembrance of Him whose body was broken and whose blood was shed. I told what his sacrifice had meant and what ours might mean if we consecrated ourselves to Him. It was a moving service.

During the day we had several alarms but nothing happened. The marvel of radar gives warning, and time to prepare. We are hoping that we may make port without incident. During the day we heard reports of fighting that made us feel we were there already. We will be soon.

It is fearfully hot tonight and I'm running with sweat as I write. I'm too stifled to think clearly. I'll shorten this letter, brief in words but long in love.

* * *

We have arrived. Things are popping but I think we will be OK. I have already had an authentic view of the real thing. More later. But don't worry if you don't hear. It takes time to get settled.

Russell

All of the letters above arrived in Lynchburg on May 12. The next letter, containing an eagerly awaited reassurance, arrived just three days later. (From this time forward, Emma wrote the arrival date on every envelope.) Stroup wrote the day before Emma's birthday, after six days of combat.

Saturday, April 29, 1944

HAPPY BIRTHDAY, MOTHER

This will be a short note as I have a chance to send one out by plane—a rare opportunity. I have written regularly but when you'll get those letters I don't know. I have had everything happen. I have tended the wounded and the dying, buried the dead (none from our own outfit, fortunately), seen a man shot not a hundred feet from me, given cold water, food, and comfort to frightened enemy prisoners, helped evacuate missionaries held prisoner by the Japanese and, along with them, women, children, and the old refugees from war. I live in the combat zone. As I write I can hear the artillery, and even rifle shots.

But I am well—and so satisfied to be of real help! The campaign has been extensive, yet with relatively few casualties. It is mostly mopping up now, so you need not worry about me.

Right now we are parked on an airfield doing an engineering job. When we started this job they were still fighting at the other end of the field, which shows how engineers work.

Tell Cranston I have plenty of good souvenirs: Jap flag, weapons, helmets, etc. I hope to get them to him. I'm OK. Don't worry, the time for that is past.

Russell

The landing at Hollandia, code-named "Reckless," was the first major assault in General MacArthur's advance toward the Philippines. His strategy was to "leapfrog" over some Japanese strongholds in order to secure bases that might, in turn, support additional, rapid, "leapfrog" advances toward his destination. The Hollandia area was selected because there were two excellent deep-water ports in the vicinity, there were beaches for landing, and Japanese airfields in the flat interior areas could be expanded to accommodate American long-range bombers. To reach Hollandia, the convoy slipped past more formidable Japanese strongholds at Wewak and Hansa Bay.

The plan of attack called for fifty-two thousand men, plus vast quantities of equipment, to be landed on the beaches during the first three days of attack. Thirty-two thousand more men would be landed subsequently. The majority were landed in Humboldt Bay, with the remainder set ashore further west at Tanahmerah Bay, where Japanese garrisons were believed to be smaller. From both directions, troops were to cross foothills of the Cyclops Mountains and converge in the Sentani Lake area in order to seize three Japanese airfields.

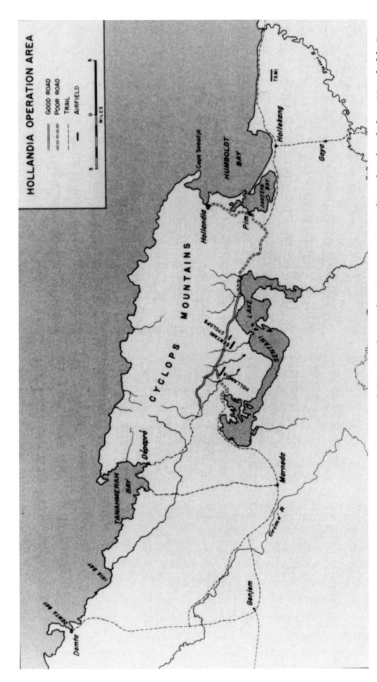

The Hollandia operation area. Stroup accompanied the 239th Combat Engineer Battalion that landed at Humboldt Bay and advanced inland to an airfield near Sentani Lake. From Smith, Approach to the Philippines, 17.

Humboldt Bay. Stroup's unit landed on "White 1" beach. The beach soon became overcrowded, with disastrous consequences. From Smith, Approach to the Philippines, *44.*

The 239th Combat Engineer Battalion landed with many other units on White Beach 1. When the first combat engineers landed on D day, Sunday, April 22, they set to work clearing the beach and attempting to construct a road inland to the existing trail connecting the village of Pim to the south with the town of Hollandia to the north. When a swamp blocked the swift completion of this task, the unit turned to assisting the unloading of other craft on the increasingly congested beach. This delay in opening a route for men and equipment to move inland added to acute overcrowding along White Beach 1 during the next two days.

Stroup's LST landed the second morning of the invasion. Because the originals of his first letters from Hollandia have been lost, I have relied on Cranston's transcriptions. These were very accurate for the letters I could compare against the originals, except that he omitted both salutation and signature.

[Sunday, April 23, 1944]

We landed on a long, curving beach that made a beautiful crescent of white sand backed by palm trees and rimmed by mountains. We came in through pounding surf, wading waist high onto the shore where many hundreds of men and piles of equipment had preceded us. To our left about one-half mile, bombs and shells were exploding in a tremendous din, although the Japanese, after slight resistance, had moved back into the hills. However, the fighting along the beach was far from finished. We drove down the sand for a couple of miles and bivouacked in a grove of trees. I continued for another mile to where all vehicles were being stopped with the warning that the front line had been reached.

There were some indications of the battle that had preceded our landing—shattered trees and burned areas that looked like a forest fire—but most of the beach looked undamaged. There were plenty of Jap pillboxes and dugouts where resistance might have been offered, but was not.

All along the beach there were "villages" that the Japanese had occupied. Peering into the thatched huts one could see how swiftly they had been evacuated. There was an oven with food in a pan and a spoon trust into it, as though the cook had paused in his stirring, and then cleared out. There were many camp areas where equipment was piled in incredible confusion. You could pick up almost anything, and most of the soldiers did. The Japs had succeeded in burning some of these installations. We picked up a melted crucifix and other sacred objects, apparently part of loot they had taken from churches. It seemed portentous to find the blackened, tortured figure of the suffering Christ, mutilated by war.

I saw the first of many dead Japanese on our landing day, sprawled in pathetic postures. Some were gruesome, but many were as men fallen asleep beside the way because it was too hard for them and they were tired. It was too early yet for burial: that must wait for the fighting to subside.

Down on the beach thousands of American boys disported in the surf. It was hard to remember you were not on a pleasure beach. In the habit of Americans, they were having a wonderful time, even in the presence of death. In the two days we remained on the beach, morning and evening dips were most refreshing. I never swam on a lovelier, more gently sloping, sandy beach.

As I made my way toward the "front" I met my first wounded Japanese, lying guarded by a soldier who was almost as frightened as the Jap, for this was his first experience. The Jap reached out a pathetic hand holding a can for water, but apparently the soldier didn't realize his need, for he paid no attention and even tried to prevent me from responding. I insisted, and for the first but not the last time I saw a grateful look in the eyes of a frightened, hurt peasant boy as I gave him water and food. "If your enemy hunger, feed him. If he thirst, give him drink." And so I have to many since then. I have tried, with gentle politeness, to help the enemy prisoners. I think they have responded as much to friendliness as to food or drink. How courteously they bow, and how they smile, half wondering, half grateful. Let no one tell you that the Japanese will not be taken prisoner. Given a chance, which under the circumstances of jungle warfare they seldom get, they will give up—and quite a number have.

The American soldiers I passed were interesting. They went to war as to a football game and came back loaded with booty. They love to put on Japanese uniforms, and a few proudly carried Samurai swords taken from officers.

On that first day I also helped to evacuate wounded Americans. I was impressed by the cheerful, jesting spirit of most of them, although with some it was necessary to give comfort and assurance—they were hurt, frightened boys.

Stroup would have been prevented by military censorship from mentioning the tragic events of that night on the beach near him. According to Robert Ross Smith's official history, The Approach to the Philippines:

> *Shortly after dark on the night of 23–24 April, a lone Japanese aircraft, apparently guided by still smoldering fires in old Japanese dumps, dropped a stick of bombs on White Beach 1. One of these bombs, landing at the edge of a Japanese ammunition dump below Pancake Hill, started a series of conflagrations which soon spread to an American gasoline dump near by and thence to other* RECKLESS *Task Force equipment. Efforts to stop the fires during the night proved fruitless, for intense heat and continuous explosions drove back troops who tried to put out the flames or salvage materiel. The fires raged all night and through much of the next day. . . . 60 percent of the rations and ammunition landed through D plus 1 was burned or blown up during the following two days. The equivalent of eleven LST loads of supplies was lost, while twenty-four men were killed and about one hundred wounded or injured as a result of the fires and explosions. (78–79)*

On the morning following the outbreak of this fire, Stroup was called away from the beach on quite a different errand.

[Monday, April 24, 1944]

I learned from the infantry that they had surprised and dispersed some Japanese who, in fleeing, left behind some of their prisoners who had been carrying their supplies. These included several score men and women, priests, nuns, and Protestant missionaries who had been captured in various regions and retained by the Japanese. They were exhausted, and some were sick, so we volunteered to send some men to help bring them down.

We climbed through a difficult jungle trail and found the first group, utterly worn out—some ill and all somewhat hysterical. They were so happy to be "recaptured" that they could hardly contain their joy. Those I talked with were Dutch, Polish, or German.

Those who could speak English told me that they had been used by the Japanese to tend gardens and, in the Japanese flight, had carried supplies. They had not been fed well, at least by our standards, but they had not been abused by torture or beating, nor had the women been molested. They had been allowed to practice their religion, to hold services, and even to minister to some of the Christian natives. They were thin, worn, and pitiful. Most of these we hoisted on ladders for their journey to safety—carried by eager Americans so happy to serve and so proud to be rescuers.

There were also quite a number of Sikh and Gurkha troops [from India], captured at Singapore, who had been kept here working for the Japanese. Their story was similar: hard work, insufficient food, in their case some harsh discipline, but none had been tortured or murdered. The Indians are fine-looking soldiers. They delight in saluting our soldiers, even our privates—much to the delight of the privates. Many speak splendid English, and our men have taken quite a liking to them. For now they are working for us, but they are eager to get a crack at the Japanese in some more militant fashion.

We all rejoiced in our mission to give freedom to those who were "bound."

[Tuesday, April 25, 1944]

This day I also spent searching for refugees, assisting a Javanese "Leftenant" who is serving with us as liaison to the local police. I took him and three scouts—one Celebes, one New Guinean, and one Javanese—in my jeep. They were all Muslims: fine fellows, so friendly and so kindly.

We found a good many refugees whose homes had been destroyed and who were wandering about between the fighting armies. They were the picture of refugees all over the world. Mothers carrying their babies and little children clinging to their skirts, crying or wide-eyed with fear. The men and the aged were burdened with the pitiful handful of possessions they could save from their meager store. All had been terrified by Japanese stories about the Americans and, of course, they had been in real danger since it is hard for a boy from America to distinguish between Orientals—they all look like Japs to him. I have done a good deal of "rescuing" since that day, as these poor folks have been scattered all through the hills. The natives we can distinguish are safe, but my heart bleeds for the others.

The first group we met were being fed and cared for by our soldiers, but they were still bewildered and frightened. Our little group of scouts was the first they had met who understood their language—how happy they were to find friends! I helped to feed them, carried bundles for grandmothers and babies for mothers, and saw faces brighten with smiles. It warmed the heart. They had no love for the Japanese, but they had not been mistreated in the extreme sense, and their lovely little women had not been harmed. Indeed, they told us that Japanese soldiers were under strict orders not to harm women, and the orders were enforced.

The fourth day we started to move to where the infantry had preceded us in their pursuit of the enemy. The road was poor and we only got a short way, so we decided to stop at the corps headquarters for the night. This was the very center of all operations, and it was interesting to see how a command operates in time of battle.

The troops there were detailed to guard the headquarters. They were nervous, as they thought that Japanese were about. So every movement in the bushes, or every shadow at night, set off a barrage of fire. It wasn't safe to take even a couple of steps after dark. My bed was right near the general's tent, so I felt fairly safe. However, shooting all night kept us wakeful.

Early the next morning I was going along a road when I heard a shot and a lot of shouting. Hurrying over I found a boy who had been shot by a sniper hidden in the trees. The men with him did what they could while others went after the sniper—whom they didn't get. We carried the wounded man to the aid station but, poor fellow, he was dead by the time we got there. There was no chaplain in his unit, so I took charge. We had a service with full military honors. His comrades were all there and, after a great deal of difficulty, we got a bugle for taps. Of course we had a firing squad. I think the service was helpful, and the commanding officer was most appreciative.

I had hardly finished the service when I heard that the commanding officer of our outfit [the 239th Combat Engineer Battalion], together with a few others, was going to try to get through to the airstrip where the fighting was going on, in order to lay plans for our work. Without asking permission I started out behind them, keeping out of sight down the road until I was far enough along to know they wouldn't send me back. I got by the MPs by saying that I was with the major, although a couple were rather skeptical about what a chaplain would be doing. It was quite a ride: right through the lines, over some very difficult road, up and around the mountains. All along the way we passed evidence of the fighting still in progress: bomb craters, artillery holes, smashed equipment, and the unburied dead—something of a nightmare. However, the mountains were lovely, and most beautiful of all was the valley into which we at last emerged. It has a peaceful blue lake reminiscent of Tahoe; quite as large and just as breathtaking. Near the shores are native settlements, on stilts in the water—very picturesque.

We got to the airstrip while the firing was still in progress. As a matter of fact we were told by some officer, at one point, that we were beyond the front lines. Our Air Corps had done an amazing job. Hundreds of enemy planes were smashed on the ground and, in consequence, there had been none to oppose our landing. Thousands of lives had been saved. Our unit's job was to prepare the fields for our planes. It was essential that we begin at once.

Our first night by the airfield was exciting, and the danger of attack kept us on alert constantly. I was awakened about five-thirty by the cries of a man standing guard, who had been hit. I got to him before the medics and did what I could to quiet him; he had a bad case of shock. Fortunately his wound, though very painful, was not serious, and we got him to a field hospital.

There I saw what my job must be for the day, so I stayed at the hospital helping to care for the wounded and the dying. There were not many of the latter, thank God. I went out to find a Catholic priest, as many of the boys were Catholics and wanted a priest. I stayed at the field hospital into the night. This must have been helpful, for the doctors were cordial and urged me to come back. Sometime I want to write more impressions of those hours in an open tent where the wounded kept coming in. All were very brave, and all so enthusiastic about the work of the medics, particularly the first-aid men and the litter-bearers, who had brought them out under enemy fire.

By the next day, through the marvel of the American Army Engineers, ambulance planes were landing on the airfield and carrying the wounded back to hospitals in the rear. From there they would be flown on to more distant bases for the best medical care. Here was a use of the airplane that justified its existence—speed means life.

During these first four days in combat Stroup found a style that would intensify in subsequent engagements. The playful risk taking that he had enjoyed during training exercises in the States now became a determination, perhaps reckless, to seek out the "action." He ministered creatively to soldiers in combat, and he was particularly alert to the needs of people beyond the

formal limits of his army responsibilities—noncombatants and the Japanese
themselves. Ever the individualist, Stroup often took his "orders" from the
Jesus of the Gospels rather than from his military superiors.

From his mother, I believe, Stroup had acquired a spiritual intensity
that led him to test himself, daily, against the standard "What would Jesus
do?" Although military censorship prevented him from writing home stories
of atrocities, subsequent letters reveal a growing anxiety about the fate of
civilians and of Japanese soldiers who wished to surrender. On behalf of this
"enemy," Stroup took unusual risks. Determined to inspire a higher standard
of conduct among the troops, he ended his second week in combat with a
striking sermon to American soldiers.

The next day, April 29, was the day Stroup was able to send out, on one of
the ambulance planes, the "Happy Birthday" letter to his mother. Four days
later, when he wrote again from the field hospital, the intensity of combat
had subsided.

[Wednesday, May 3, 1944]

I have been to the hospital each day, but today I rejoice in an
opportunity to just sit and talk with some remaining boys who are
not very sick, and with attendants who are taking their first breathing
spell from hours of intense labor. There are no more blood-soaked
beds or active operating tables.

The paper on which I write was taken from Japanese headquarters.
There were many installations around here, and the American soldier
is an incurable souvenir hunter. He will stop in the midst of battle to
gather up anything and everything and risk his life going close to the
enemy to retrieve treasured objects. I have seen soldiers loaded down
with stuff—they would refuse to carry so much if ordered. They go
about dressed in uniform combinations: half Japanese, half American.
I have gathered my share, but whether I will be able to get it home I
don't know. I have a Japanese helmet; I could have a hundred. I have a
Japanese flag, such as every soldier carries, with the names of his friends
inscribed on it. I have an Enfield rifle, taken by the Japanese from the
Hindus, used by them, and recovered by me. I have a parachute in its
case, the purest of Japanese silk. I have some very fine hammered brass
pans that I'm using for washbasins.

If this sounds like a lot, you should see some of the men. Some
have picked up knickknacks like Ford sedans, Chevrolet trucks, etc.,
of which the Japanese were rather well supplied. Between trucks,

The Japanese soldier's flag that Stroup sent to his brother measured twenty-seven inches in height between the ties, and thirty-two inches in width.

steamrollers, half-tracks, motorcycles, and the bicycles that the infantry that arrived first on the field gathered up, they practically became mechanized. It looks very American to see a bunch of soldiers on patrol puttering over a pile of junk they have somehow managed to get started and are driving about. The problem of gas rationing doesn't present itself as there are thousands of drums of Japanese gasoline scattered about, from which the boys draw liberally. This was quite a supply depot for this part of the world.

The Japanese encampments were in lovely spots in the hills, with plenty of trees and flowing streams. I am struck by the amazing number of books, magazines, etc., they had about. There are no characteristic American pinup pictures, or at least only a few, but many photographs and pictures of the home folks and the homeland—whole albums, which must be hard for them to part with. It seems strange to me that I have found only a couple indications of shrines. In some of the officers' huts they had little Japanese gardens made in the burls of trees. All about are vegetable gardens, indeed some rather extensive farming. I have gathered cucumbers, tomatoes, turnips, lettuce, and peanuts from their fields. Apparently each man did his own cooking, for there are no large cooking utensils but many small ones, and their little bowls are everywhere.

They were plentifully supplied with sake, beer, etc., which have not been overlooked by the souvenir hunters—often with painful results. They had a lot of baseball equipment, also fencing masks and armor. Within their camps, apparently, they put on their slippers, and even kimonos. Almost every hut has pictures of the cherry blossoms and the temples of home.

. . . The campaign has not been without difficulties, and there are mental strains that are more difficult than the physical. I have been through literal hells of emotion during this week. I am sometimes thankful, for their sake, that so many men are not more imaginative, but for everyone this is a heart-wringing experience. There is so much I want to do, but cannot, for no one can alter the hideous face of war.

[Thursday, May 4, 1944]

At last I have my typewriter in some kind of shape and will be able to write with a little more ease. It got quite a beating coming up here.

Since the first few days things have settled down. The opposition is back in the hills, and mopping up parties are doing most of the fighting. I don't think the Japanese have much fight left in them. As a matter of fact they have been coming in as best they can to give themselves up. That isn't easy, for our men have jumpy trigger fingers. It is a fortunate Nipponese who can get near enough to give up. Yesterday, orders went out to bring in as many prisoners as possible, so from now on there may be more of them.

As a matter of fact, I have spent the past few days riding around close to the hills where Japanese have been seen, hoping that some of them—seeing me by myself and unarmed—might surrender to me. But so far I have had no luck and no prisoners. I arrived some places just too late, but I have not given up hope and continue to look. A good many of the men brought in, whom I have visited at the prisoner-of-war stockades, are Koreans from labor battalions. These Koreans have little affection for the Japanese. Then there are many farmers and fishermen that the Japanese brought here to provision the soldiers.

They are boys and old men, not fighting forces, and my sympathies have gone out to them.

The prisoners have been pumped full of propaganda. Most think that we will be unable to go back home since Japanese forces have captured Washington State, Oregon, and California. They have heard about no Japanese defeats, and it is hard for them to comprehend that we are here. I think that most believe we are desperately seeking refuge where we can find it, since our escape from destruction is cut off.

The effects of the great fire on White Beach 1 were still being felt by the American troops.

Often our supplies have been short, but I think we will soon be on regular rations. We do our own cooking, for the kitchens have not caught up with us. There are three kinds of rations: K-rations that you eat only when you can get nothing else; C-rations that are a little better, being cans of cheese, egg yolk and ham, corned beef, and hardtack with soluble coffee or extract of lemonade; and finally there are ten-in-one rations, which are packaged in boxes intended to serve a squad of men. These are pretty fancy: canned beef, canned corn, canned tomatoes, pork sausage, dehydrated corned beef, dehydrated baked beans that are very much like those Bean Hole Beans we used to buy, and a delicious pudding of rice and pineapple. Also in these rations are a better biscuit, canned butter, canned milk and jam, with coffee as well. Oh yes, there is also a cereal of whole wheat and soybeans with powdered milk, salt, and sugar, to which you simply add hot water to make a cooked cereal that is not half bad. If you can get hold of ten-in-one by hook or crook you are most fortunate, and my man Eleanor [the chaplain's assistant] has been pretty successful so far.

We have rigged up a stove out of sheet aluminum and use Jap gasoline for fuel. I haven't suffered from lack of food and I doubt if any of the men have, although there have been a good many complaints.

I have slept in a jungle hammock since the beginning of the operation. A lot of men began by sleeping in foxholes, but I was not that apprehensive and preferred to be comfortable. I brought a folding cot in my trailer. I set that up with my rubber mattress, and put my jungle hammock on top of that. It has its own mosquito bar, so I have been quite comfortable at night. I would have slept well were it not for the firing at night, and for the memories from the day that are often not conducive to repose.

It has been a godsend to have my jeep and trailer. I think I'm the only chaplain hereabouts who has one, which puts me in an enviable position. It gives me the opportunity to contact a great many scattered units that have no chaplains of their own and are in situations where they needed one.

Although it has been scarcely two weeks since we started this operation, I am ready for a rest, but doubt that I will get one. The work will go on. We will be constructing airfields and roads, and there remains plenty to do to put the place in shape.

Stroup writes a little more candidly about the fact that he has created a situation where he can make his own decisions.

I am not sure what my status will be. Perhaps the [1112th Engineer] Group will catch up with me here. Of course it was never contemplated that a single battalion should have a chaplain, as is the case now. I do serve where I can with other troops but, since the corps or division chaplains have not caught up with us yet, what I have done has been on my own and without authority from above.

We have quite a flock of planes going in and out of here now, and I think the pilots are rather hoping that the Japs will try a raid just so they can get into action. I have a big bombproof shelter handy: the Japs once stored bombs there, but with the bombs removed the shelter will serve our whole company. That saved us the work of digging foxholes.

The "shelter" a few paces from Stroup's hammock was, in fact, a hazard until all Japanese bombs were removed, which had not yet been accomplished. From here forward, Stroup's original letters are again available.

Friday, May 5, 1944

Dearest Mother and Cranston,

I do know that this is Friday and I think the fifth. There has been much to write about that I have little heart to set down.

We go to sleep at night with guards posted and the surrounding area protected by booby traps. They string wires through the trees and underbrush. These are attached to hand grenades or dynamite charges. If anyone, friend or foe, stumbles against them in the night the charge goes off. The other night a bull went against one such and, when the remains were discovered in the morning, there wasn't enough meat left for a meal.

As I write, artillery is shelling the hills behind us where nests of resistance persist. Last night we had an air-raid alert, but no raid. About twenty-five feet from my hammock is a Japanese storehouse for aerial bombs—several hundred big fellows. The men had been carting them away in trucks as they had time, but the alert last night really got men to work: they moved the bombs in a hurry lest a lucky hit on the dump dispose of all of us. If the air raid alert did nothing else, it got rid of the bombs around here.

We don't have tents, but yesterday my assistant Eleanor brought in practically a whole hut. I'm sitting here tonight in luxury, the envy of our command and of many others who come by just to see the wonder. The hut is nine by twelve with a wood floor, thatched palm sides, and a roof of sheet aluminum. Inside there is a complete covering of Japanese mosquito netting; the place is practically impervious to bugs. It is watertight, insect tight, reptile tight—quite fancy!

To add to the amazement, our men found a small, working Japanese electric plant that they set up this afternoon. They placed a bulb in the main headquarters and in each company headquarters and, just to show respect, one in the chaplain's new quarters. So I actually have electric lights. Of course this makes me a good target, but I hope that there are no Japanese in the bushes. When you are in an engineering outfit with plenty of skilled workers you can get fixed pretty comfortably. It is odd that this shack—the most permanent and comfortable quarters I've had—is right on the front lines.

I ran into my Javanese friends today. I happened to be with a group of infantrymen and their chaplain when the jeep full of Javanese, Celebes, and native scouts drove up. When they all piled out and pressed around me to shake my hand it caused a commotion of surprise among the infantry that I should be a bosom companion of such strange-looking soldiers. I'm going to make the most of my opportunity and do some scouting with the leftenant, to get to know some of the natives. . . .

We have had no letters now for almost three weeks and it looks like we'll have to wait even longer.

Russell

Sunday, May 7, 1944

Dearest family,

A peaceful and helpful Sabbath day was marred a moment ago, as I sat down to write, by the snarling staccato of machine-gun fire not far away. I don't like the sound that speaks so eloquently of pain and death. It is hard to get used to being where suffering and slaughter are the commonplace of every day, and returning squads say in an offhand manner, "Got three more Japs in the hills today," or "One of our men caught it on patrol." Perhaps it is a blessing that men can take it so—nature's way of deadening a shock too great for the mind to bear.

I preached today on the Sermon on the Mount: "Ye have heard that it was said by them of old time, Thou shalt not kill; and whosoever shall kill shall be in danger of judgment: But I say to you, That whosoever is angry with his brother without cause shall be in danger of the judgment: and whosoever shall say to his brother, Raca, shall be in danger of the counsel: but whosoever shall say, Thou fool, shall be in danger of hell fire" [Matt. 5:21–22].

Knowing Stroup, I can imagine him preaching that it is not the killing we are required to do that endangers our souls so much as hatred for the enemy, the anger that we allow to well up within us, and fear that blocks humane actions.

It wasn't an easy message to bring out here, but I thought it was needed and I made it as strong as I could. I want desperately that these men shall return home with as few spiritual scars as is possible under the circumstances—for their own sake in the days of peace, and for the future that they must build on a sure foundation. They will be better soldiers if they can hear this message, and certainly better men back home.

There were two services for this battalion as our men are working three shifts, day and night. Then I had another service for an aviation engineers battalion that has a Catholic but no Protestant chaplain. They were most appreciative and made me promise to return.

The day did me good. I needed Sunday, and yet I had dreaded its approach, for "How shall we sing the Lord's song in a strange land?" [Ps. 137:4].

The mail still has not come through. It has been hard enough to get rations in so we have been getting by on rather slim, monotonous fare. There are several boys who get together to cook their meals and they always have something for the chaplain, so I am better served than most. This includes officers, for the men won't cook for officers if they can help it—but they don't put the chaplain in that category.

Stroup concluded the letter by hinting that he might soon be reunited with the 111 2th Combat Engineer Group, which remained on Goodenough Island but would probably move quickly to a new assault.

I would very much like to give the men of the Twenty-seventh the advantage of my experience. I think I could forestall some of the mistakes we have made here.

Russell

Thursday, May 11, 1944

Dearest Mother and Cranston,

I have a lot to write and not much time, so I'll do the best I can. Monday, having heard that the [1112th] Group was somewhere on the beach where we landed so many days ago, I decided to go down and contact them. A warrant officer, a driver, and I set out by jeep over a bad road, much worse than when I came up it, due to the heavy traffic. When we could drive no further we sent the driver back and proceeded on foot. We walked a couple of miles across boggy country until we reached a real swamp where we took off our shoes and wallowed through. It was hard going and it took us from early morning until evening to travel the twenty miles. The last part of our journey was over the bay by boat, and we arrived just after supper.

At the Group camp I managed to get some supper. They had fresh rolls and other food such as I had been dreaming about for weeks, so I gorged myself. The evening was spent catching up with my old friends, now together again and with a job in prospect. They want me back with them. It is possible I will be transferred back very soon. This will mean another adventure, hard after the one I just finished, but I would like to be with them. Things are now pretty stable here, and there are now plenty of chaplains to serve all troops in this vicinity.

The best thing about the visit was that I got my mail, which they had been holding for me—thirty or forty letters.

Stroup suddenly deflected to a story weighing on his mind. Apparently, when he encountered bodies of victims, he did his best to bury the Japanese soldiers as well as the American.

One day, when I was looking for bodies to bury, I came across a dead Japanese soldier. He had fallen on the bank of a little stream with his head and shoulders in the water. Sitting near his head, in the water, was a yellow dog, looking very lonely—way up in the hills with no one around. He sat gazing down at his master, who must have lain there for at least a night and a day. When I tried to approach the dog arose and bared his fangs. I tried in every way to persuade him that I was a friend, but I could not lure him away. The poor thing must have been hungry, but the food I offered him was no bribe. He still stood guard. I didn't want to shoot the dog, and I saw no other way to approach his master, so finally I had to go away. I left some food behind for the dog and planned to return. However, when I was able to do so, both dog and master were gone and some troops were camped near the site. I imagine they solved the problem in their own way.

Some people don't like dogs, but I'm partial to them. In war you find so many looking out for No. 1; it is good to find someone who's faithful.

Apparently, Stroup returned to his camp near the airstrip on Tuesday.

Wednesday I spent with my friend the Javanese leftenant, one of his men, and a Dutch captain. It was a great experience. Captain Boot, pronounced Boat, was a six-foot-two blond giant with a fine physique and a handsome face. He had been an aviator in the Netherlands East Indian Army. I enjoyed the time spent with him for he is a good conversationalist, the best I've met recently.

I drove them in my jeep down to the lake where a native chief of three villages was waiting with a forty-foot "prau," or canoe. It was carved from a single giant tree and beautifully decorated with elaborate handwork that made it look much more elegant than the simple dugout it really was. In the center they had placed two little bamboo chairs for the white "tuans" to sit on. Distinctions were made: the captain and I as white men were given the chairs, the Javanese leftenant and his man were given boards across the canoe, the native chief stood, and twelve men did the paddling.

The captain and the leftenant both spoke Malay, understood here by the better-educated natives. Since they also spoke excellent English, I had fine interpreters and learned much about the natives.

The chief was headman of three villages, a small but dignified man with an excellent sense of humor. When he laughed he revealed his red, ragged teeth and gaping red mouth, both discolored by betel nut, which they all chew. He and his men were dressed in odds and ends of

Japanese and American clothes, but the chief's badge of authority—or perhaps crown—was a bright plaid golf cap which he had received from the Dutch in the distant past.

We departed with a great deal of shouting, which accompanies everything the natives do. Our voyage across the lake took about two hours and a half. This beautiful lake is surrounded by high mountains and bordered by deep forests. Along the shores and on the islands there are native villages, usually built on stilts over the water—for protection, I presume. Their gardens are inland.

They also do a great deal of fishing, and the stakes that mark their fishnets are everywhere. I inquired about some that we were passing, so the chief obligingly stopped the boat and called to native women and children in a nearby village. They came out in canoes to put on a fish hunt for me. Poles hold the net. The natives gather in a circle around it and, with much shouting and beating of the water, converge on the net driving the fish before them. When they reach the net they gather in the ends and pull it out loaded, they hope, with fish. We watched the procedure with interest. Late that evening when we stopped at that same village on our return, one of the village men brought me a little woven palm basket filled with fish they had caught that morning.

The very small children that swarm their villages wear nothing. The ones a little older wear abbreviated loincloths. The men, except for those who have Jap or American clothes, wear loincloths. The women wear a wrapped-around sarong that covers them from the waist down. The people are generally dark and Negroid.

The villages are composed of large houses on piles—a hundred feet or more in length and twenty to thirty feet in width—made of woven palm. Each houses a large clan. In one that I visited there were 147 men, women, and children—I took no census of the dogs that were everywhere. There were no windows and only a few doors. Here they live, eat, and sleep. They build fires in the middle of the floor, either on a large flat stone or on very hard wood that won't burn, and here they cook. Smoke finds its way out the best it can; most of it seems to stay inside. It is very crowded, noisy, smoky, and dirty.

Protestant missionaries have been quite active in this section, German and Dutch mostly. Each village, consisting of seven hundred to a thousand persons, has a church—very nice ones with steeples. The churches also serve as schools. The best house in the village, different from the native houses, belongs to the local schoolteacher, who might be an educated native, a Malaysian, a Javanese, or an Indo-Chinese.

Most of the natives, except for the older ones, have biblical names, for when the child is brought to the mission to be baptized the missionary names him or her. The names are German or Dutch versions since such were the missionaries. You hear a list of their names, as I did, and it sounds like the concordance to the Scripture.

Some distance from our destination we met a duck, an amphibian two-and-a-half-ton truck, that came out to investigate what we were doing. It gave us a tow to our landing, to the great delight of our natives because they didn't have to row and because they had never traveled so fast in their "prau." They sat on the sides waving their paddles and shouting at the top of their lungs, lest any of the villages we passed might fail to notice their novel means of transport. The chief stood aft looking very proud, and all of us felt like celebrities riding down Wall Street with admiring crowds on the side.

We were headed for the Civil Administration Headquarters, which was on the site of an old Christian mission—a delightful spot on the shore of the lake. However, our troops had discovered it and were moving in, which damaged some of its picturesqueness. We landed amid excitement and made our way to headquarters accompanied by a crowd of natives, curious and respectful. The civil administrator is a young Netherlands officer as handsome as a movie star—very cultured, very engaging, quite religious, and an idealist who takes his work seriously. He also has a good sense of humor.

His task is to adjudicate disagreements that natives have among themselves or with the Americans, and also to recruit labor battalions necessary for our work here. The latter is not easy, for natives are not fond of structured work, especially right now, because they have gathered a plentiful harvest of supplies from fleeing Japanese and from generous Americans.

I had luncheon with the civil administrator, the resident Dutch captain, and a Dutch newspaper correspondent. The Javanese meal included rice curried with fish, good coffee, American K-rations that I refused, and delicious Papua fruit. The curry was highly spiced with a tiny red pepper, but good.

When I told of my adventures in this operation the captain observed that either I was very fortunate or a great prevaricator, since no one else he talked with had seen or experienced as much as I. The secret, of course, is that I go looking for the unusual, and also that I recognize it when I see it.

The civil administrator held court after lunch. Most of the native chiefs of this section were gathered in a large hut. Grievances had accumulated because the Japanese made no effort to mediate native affairs. Now only the white "tuan" can straighten them out.

Two chiefs stood before the white tuan's table, each claiming, with many gestures and stories, to be the village head. The tuan asked questions, interrogated other chiefs and also natives from the village, and examined old records. When he made his decision everyone was satisfied.

The next case concerned a village where troops had bivouacked and cut down the natives' trees, their livelihood. Our government had offered restitution, and the question was how to divide it. This required the wisdom of Solomon, for in such a grove each tree belonged to an individual native, and some trees are better than others. The natives are not communists. Each man made his claim, extolling the merits of his particular tree above all the others. This took considerable time, and, of course, the trees were gone so the tuan had difficulty evaluating the claims.

These deliberations were interrupted by a tremendous din toward the lake. I saw a crowd of natives surrounding a Japanese soldier with horn-rimmed glasses—small, thin, and exhausted. The natives were having sport with him, shouting choice bits that drew gales of laughter from the rest. They brought him to us. The native who was his proud captor had been tending a garden on the other side of the lake when the soldier, who had wandered two weeks in the forest, approached to ask for food. This was given. The soldier then offered to pay the native to paddle him to the far end of the lake where he believed he could find comrades and escape to Japanese-held territory. The artful native agreed, but warned the solder that many American planes flew low over the lake, and boats passed by, so it would be safer to lie in the bottom of the canoe covered with a mat. This seemed exceedingly discrete to the son of Nippon, and down in the bottom he got, was covered with the mat, and soon went to sleep to dream sweet dreams of escape. The native paddled in the opposite direction toward the headquarters, where he awakened the astonished soldier and handed him over to his enemies.

Our court continued with other cases. One problem was American soldiers who enter native villages on souvenir hunts. One chief explained, "When Japanese come to village all the men come out with spears and make much noise and look very fierce and Japanese, being very little man, he runs away, but Americans great giants and they come and we look fierce and make much noise and they laugh and give us cigarettes. Cigarettes are good, but let Americans give us cigarettes outside village." The civil administrator promised to take their complaint to the U.S. Army.

Other natives were concerned that their church had been bombed and destroyed in the fight. They wanted it rebuilt; the village suffered a terrible humiliation in not having a church. The civil administrator suggested that they get the wood and rebuild the church on the concrete foundation still there. But with devastating logic the natives pointed out that the Americans had destroyed the church, the Americans had plenty of wood, why should they work to get wood when it should be given to them by the Americans who (and this showed what amazing people the Americans are) even used nice cut wood to build latrines that are quite unessential. I'm not sure that this question was settled.

On our return we transported a second chief to his village. Both chiefs were most cordial. Through an interpreter each assured me that he would at the earliest convenience present me with some valuable token of his esteem for which he would expect nothing in return unless it should happen that the great tuan had some worthless something in the splendor of his house that he was thinking of disposing of anyhow but might decide instead to give it to the chief who would treasure it not for its intrinsic worth but for the tender associations it held for the time spent with the great tuan and because he could exhibit it to all envious men as a sign that he counted among his friends so mighty a person. We shall see what comes of all this. So ended the day.

Stroup's own ventures beyond the front lines seeking to encourage the Japanese to surrender to him had proved futile, but he inspired others to become more receptive toward taking prisoners.

I haven't yet written of the Japanese prisoner I got. Knowing how vainly I had been looking, one of our men brought me a prisoner. The soldier had been working on the road at night and, during a rest period, fell asleep in the cab of his truck. He was awakened when the truck door opened and a Japanese soldier stared in. Exhibiting rare self-control and courage, our man neither bolted nor shot the intruder but realized that he had come to give himself up. He brought the Jap in and, just as I was going to bed, turned him over to me as a gift.

We named the Jap "Charlie." He was little more than a boy, hungry and frightened, feet and legs covered with sores and blisters. A bunch of men gathered around. We offered Charlie food, but, hungry as he was, he would eat nothing until we had sampled it first. He kept asking for rice, and when we told him we had none he couldn't believe that anyone with food would lack the staff of life. Nevertheless, he was appreciative, and he captivated the men by his apparent lack of fear. For instance, when we, using a Japanese phrase book, asked him what his occupation was, he answered with illustrative gestures that it was shooting Americans. Someone produced Japanese money with a picture of Mount Fuji on it and, suggesting that it was worthless paper, made as though to tear it up. Charlie snatched it from him and reverently touched the picture of the sacred mountain to his forehead, bowing his head. Then, for the first time, tears flowed down his cheeks.

Before all this we had taken Charlie to the dispensary to treat his sores. One of the aid men was most kindly. This fine young boy knelt with me in front of the Jap, and while I bathed his feet he treated and bandaged them. Not only was Charlie a "hated enemy" but his feet were very dirty and the sores were nasty and runny. But our aid man treated him as gently as one of our own men—and that in front of a crowd of his comrades who did not praise such activity.

The American soldier is not naturally cruel. Once all the men got to know Charlie, they continued to have fun with him, which he seemed to enjoy, but they were very decent. I think his presence will have a good effect. It is fortunate that Charlie is spunky, because Americans admire that trait even in an enemy. He said and did things that I would not have the courage to do if captured by the Japanese.

Russell

The rescue and protection of those who wished to surrender would remain an important theme in Stroup's ministry.

A few days after mailing the preceding letter, which was so long that it had to be mailed in two envelopes, Stroup was formally detached from the 239th Combat Engineer Battalion at the airfield, in order to return to the 1112th Engineer Group, now on the beach at Hollandia. He wrote his brother, who had recently entered a period of remission, with the encouragement that led Cranston to begin transcribing the letters. Stroup then articulated his emerging role as a chaplain, justifying his adventuresomeness with the thought that it might get him home sooner.

Dear Cranston,

I have a lot of packing to do because tomorrow, after Sunday service here, I start out to report to the Group. . . .

It's good news to me that you have written some short stories. I hope that you will keep it up. In some of the stuff I've written home there might be inspiration—anything you want is yours. That only goes for you, not for others. I hope you can find something.

I am anxious to get into as many operations as possible, and I think that I have a good chance to be a kind of roving chaplain. This will greatly increase my experience and, as I have suggested, possibly hasten my return. For after I have been through several campaigns I'll not hesitate to suggest that I have done my part out here and should be used elsewhere, giving someone back home a chance at foreign service.

Russell

On the beach, Stroup now worked under the direct supervision of the chief chaplain of the division. This situation made him restless. Although it was too soon for his family to have received the letters written during combat and responded, Cranston, knowing his brother, wrote to express concern that he might take unnecessary chances. Realizing how much he had already written home, Stroup did his best to offer belated reassurance.

Dear Cranston,

These are lazy days of recuperation and preparation and they go sliding by with little to mark their passage until of a sudden you discover it is Sunday and a week has gone by. Tomorrow I'll have a service with an outfit strange to me, working under the direction of the chief chaplain of the division to which our Group is attached. There are not enough in our Group to justify a separate service and, pending the arrival of the engineering units which will operate under the Group's direction and be our charges, we will serve the division. This constant shifting, with always new groups to deal with, is not my preference but it seems to be my lot. I try to make the best of it. It does take some zest out of the work. Rather, it shifts the emphasis: I begin to think of the varied experiences I may get that will be of value in the future rather than progressive work with a group of men, as I had once envisioned. Of course I can make some impression, much as one does in summer camps or at religious emphasis weeks at colleges. . . .

You mention the matter of me taking undue chances. I should say that mighty few out here do. They are not supposed to, and their own inclinations jibe with their instructions. The strategy out here is to accomplish maximum results with minimum casualties, and so far we have been successful in this. With decent caution, which most of us exhibit, and with any kind of luck, there is no good reason why anything should happen to me.

I try to give you a vivid impression of my experiences, and there is always the danger that I overstress the dramatic dangers and so give a false picture. It is rather like driving a car at home. You go on for miles and miles without incident, and then every once and a while you have a close shave that might have caused an accident but usually doesn't. In fact, one's feelings are somewhat the same. There is no fear in the moment as you are too busy getting through, and then afterwards there comes a sinking feeling due to realization of what might have been. But most of it is just driving along observing safety rules automatically, or with conscious care, and with little real peril. This is not meant to ease your mind but to give you the straight dope.

Russell

The 1112th Combat Engineers and many other units were now camped on the beach, awaiting the call to load transports for the next "leapfrog" assault. Stroup's last letter from Hollandia is reflective.

Wednesday, May 24, 1944

Dearest family,

You remember in the last war the high enthusiasm of the men who went away and of those who stayed behind. It was the spirit of [Phillips] Brooks's poem,

"Now God be thanked who has matched us with His hour."

Ours was a crusade, and we were consecrated to a high endeavor that found expression in the words of Wilson as he spoke of a war to end war, a war against tyranny, a war to make the world safe for

Democracy. Afterwards came the disillusionment which those of us who hated war did our part to foster. We scoffed at the idea that there were any principles involved or that the men who died had given their lives for freedom or for peace. Ours was a sincere desire to debunk war and show it for the bestial thing which it is, but we missed something which we should have known.

What men die for is not necessarily what they achieve. It is one thing to say that the war did not accomplish the high purposes to which men were dedicated and another thing to say that these did not fight and die for an ideal. I think now that they did, and I think that somehow their consecration gave dignity and worth to their sacrifice.

But we made men cynical, and when another conflict came you could no longer fire men with thrilling phrases or fill them with a sense of their high purpose. They scoffed, as they had learned to scoff, at all such quixotic nonsense. So we accomplished the greatest tragedy of this war: that men go out to die unsustained by any consciousness of fighting for ideals so great and worthy—much bigger than we—that life might be found in the losing of it for their sake.

While I believe with all my heart that freedom, decency, and brotherhood are not secured through war, I do believe that their destruction may be averted by opposing force with force. This seems to be the only method we have had the wisdom to devise. I feel with all my heart that this is a time of revolution when the whole world is divided between antagonistic philosophies of life. Both cannot live in the same world. As Lincoln insisted that a nation could not remain half slave and half free, so there can be no peace in humanity so long as some men conceive of the good life in terms of materialism, regimentation, brute force, and blood and iron. There can be no freedom for any unless there is freedom for all. There can be no security anywhere unless there is security everywhere.

It is true that we who believe in liberty, human personality, democracy, and the more abundant life will not achieve our ideals thorough conflict. But it is equally true that the opposite philosophy would by its very nature be justified by victory through force. Since they have insisted that their way of life finds its highest expression in war, and that right is determined by might (and that is the Fascist philosophy whether in Germany or in America), then to defeat them by the very means which is their pride would do much to convince them of the fatal fallacy of their position.

To that extent there is a method in this madness. The victory of our philosophy must be achieved in peace, but the defeat of their philosophy can be accomplished through war.

These are some of the thoughts that have been engaging me as I sit here remembering the recent past and contemplating an uncertain future. I have felt so keenly that lack in our fighting forces. Men need a high purpose to uphold them in any undertaking that demands the best that they have to give. You remember, I used to say that we had raised a generation that had found nothing worth living for and certainly nothing for which they would be willing to die and, as a wiser one than I said a long time ago, men never learn to live until they have found something for which they are willing to die.

How fortunate I am, for I not only have an appreciation of the issues involved, but in addition I have a work which in itself would be reason enough to sacrifice. I truly can work "for God and Country." . . . There is so much to do. I just interrupted this letter to deal with a man in some other outfit who had gone temporarily out of his mind because he had received news of his father's death. Such tragedies are doubly hard out here, so very far from home. Here is a man with two brothers in the army and a mother and father left at home. His father dies, and of course he is deeply concerned for a mother who has no one to sustain her. Of course he is in a highly emotional state.

Evident in Stroup's letter is an awareness—which he cannot share directly —that the next day they will board ships to begin a new assault.

Last night I had a request from an engineering outfit nearby to conduct a service for them, and once more I used the text "Be strong, be of good courage, be not dismayed, neither be thou afraid, for the Lord thy God is with thee whithersoever thou goest." We sang "How firm a Foundation" with assurance, and then "Jesus, lover of my soul." . . .

Other refuge have I none, hangs my helpless soul on Thee.
Leave, ah, leave me not alone, Still support and comfort me.
All my trust on Thee is stayed, All my help from Thee I bring,
Cover my defenseless head with the shadow of Thy wing.

They were gracious in their insistence that the service was helpful, and I know it was for me. How wonderful it is to have a God who is able to supply all our needs. We all read together, "The Lord is my Shepherd, I shall not want. He maketh me to lie down in green pastures, he leadeth me beside the still waters, he restoreth my soul. He leadeth me in the paths of righteousness for his name's sake. Yea, though I walk through the valley of the shadow of death I shall fear no evil for Thou art with me." I closed with the Psalm that has meant to much to me since we left San Francisco, "Whither shall I go from Thy Spirit? Or whither shall I flee from thy presence? If I ascend into heaven Thou art there. If I make my bed in hell, behold Thou art there."

I think that God has a good work for me to do. These days have been preparation for that work: my forty days and nights in the wilderness. We are going to make a day, please God, when they shall neither hurt nor destroy in all God's holy mountain, but every man shall sit under his own vine and fig tree and no one shall make him afraid. To that I have dedicated myself. . . .

This must be all for now, and perhaps for a while. My dearest love to you all,

Russell

4

"Shelled, Bombed, Strafed, and Generally Annoyed Day and Night"

On May 25, the troops were loaded on transport ships. That evening, they began the five-hundred-mile journey to Biak Island in the mouth of Geelvink Bay near the western tip of New Guinea. Control of Biak was critical to General MacArthur's plans for a rapid advance toward the Philippines and the Japanese mainland, for the Japanese had constructed three major airfields there. The invasion was planned for May 27 and 28. The goal was to capture the airfields quickly and rehabilitate them so they might be used to provide air support for the next major assault of the Pacific war, the attack on the Mariana Islands planned for June 15.

Stroup apparently got his wish to be "a kind of roving chaplain." He went ashore on Saturday, May 27, the first day of the invasion, with the 162d Infantry Regiment, 41st Division. After landing at Bosnek Beach, the regiment set up a field hospital and the other facilities mentioned in the letters that follow. During the first day, the troops encountered no resistance, prompting MacArthur's headquarters to release a premature communiqué proclaiming "the practical end of the New Guinea campaign." However, Japanese troops, with artillery and light tanks, were entrenched on a strategic hillside overlooking the road to the airports. Thousands more were on another hillside overlooking the principal airport. They waited for the Americans to find them.

Biak was a tangle of coral ridges pockmarked with caves and covered with a towering jungle. It was hot. Since heavy rains disappeared underground through the fissured coral, there were no reliable water sources except one, which was within the Japanese defensive position. During the campaign most soldiers were infected with scrub typhus, a jungle disease causing headaches and high fever.

On the second day, American infantry moving toward the airports encountered stiff resistance. Soon a virtual stalemate developed. As the advance bogged down and soldiers became discouraged, Stroup visited units below the hills where the Japanese were entrenched, but his principal duties were back at the field hospital. Fighting was fierce, and the American casualties were high: sixteen killed and eighty-seven wounded on May 28, another sixteen killed and ninety-six wounded on May 29, and six killed and seventeen wounded on May 30 and 31.

Thursday, June 1, 1944

Dearest family,

There has been little time to write in the crowded days since I started less than a week ago in this campaign. I am unharmed with my morale high due to inspiration from the men with whom I've worked. I have been in wonderful ways protected by a Providence who must be moved by your prayers in my behalf. For that I am grateful, although I have a guilty feeling of special privilege not accorded to so many men who have suffered or died.

This has not been like the preceding campaign. There has been much greater opposition and still is. Then too I got in at the beginning of this one, which makes a difference. We have been shelled, bombed, strafed, and generally annoyed day and night and have spent almost as much time in foxholes as out of them. . . . Much of my time has been spent burying the dead and comforting the wounded. The latter have been superb in their spirit. The American soldier never shows up better than when he is facing stiff opposition, or when he is wounded. What grand men they are! . . .

In addition to this brief, handwritten note, Stroup found time at his typewriter later that same day to compose a more detailed report.

Since I have spent a good deal of time in the hospitals up here it would be of interest for you to know something about them. They are set up close to the front. We had artillery firing over us constantly, airplanes bombing and strafing around us, and the noise of firing at the front constant in our ears. In fact one of the hard things is to quiet the nerves of men who have been wounded under fire and cannot at the hospital get away from the crash of shells. . . .

The wards are large tents containing a couple dozen beds which are simply canvas cots or litters placed on the sand floor. Around the tents are piled sandbags to protect against flying fragments of bombs or shells. Of course nothing would protect against direct hits, but we have luckily had none. There can be no lights in the tents at night, which makes it difficult to care for the patients. The operating "rooms," also tents, are more dug out, protected, and lightproof, which makes it possible to continue operating all night long—they usually do. At night you try to quiet the apprehension of the men when there is a raid. It helps them to feel that you are there and apparently unconcerned (although I can assure you that it is only apparent). They would like to crawl into foxholes, but of course they can't. I'd like to, too, but of course I can't. So I stand there in the darkness and kid them along with a line of chatter that goes on and on. Each night before they try to sleep, I go from ward to ward and have a word of prayer. But during a raid itself they might resent prayer as seeming to express fear, so I make my prayers in jokes and chatter.

Day and night the jeeps and trucks pour in carrying the litters and we take them, wounded and weary, suffering from their hurts and the long difficult ride in on jolting vehicles. The blood drips from the litters as we lift them down. They have had what first aid was possible under fire, and so busy it is at the hospital that sometimes this must do for the less serious, for a long time.

Most of the men are incredibly, heartbreakingly cheerful. They laugh while they wince with pain. They grin through set teeth. They kid and joke in the shadow of death. . . . The American refuses to treat anything tragically, certainly not his own suffering. My job is to cheer them up, but they cheer me.

I go up and down the line of cots talking with the men of home. "Sure I know Indiana, a great state." "Yes, I've rafted down the coast of Oregon and there's no place lovelier in the whole world." "You from Ohio? I was born and raised there." "Boy, you sound like you're from the South. I'm from Virginia myself." And so it goes. They tell of their experiences at the front, how they got their wounds. A good many are wounded by shrapnel on the buttocks since they were lying in foxholes when the mortar fire hit them, and these wounds cause a lot of amusement. "Where are you going to pin your Purple Heart, over the wound?"

One lad shows me that his wound is on the identical spot on his leg where he got a piece of shrapnel at Salamaua. He can't get over the fact that he was hit twice in the same spot. Several are twice wounded. One boy asks me to care for his Purple Heart, which he had been carrying with him when he was wounded again. Now he'll have an oak leaf with the former decoration. The one thing that concerns them all is "Have I got a ticket home?" That's more important than the Purple Heart. "Chaplain, do you think they'll send us home?" from one lad—and from another, "Hell, no, you won't go home. They can't fight this war without this division."

Especially they want to know from me if I have news of some of their comrades. They have seen men hit and don't know how badly. Have I run into —— or —— and how are they doing? Their only worry seems to be for others and for the folks back home. "Chaplain, will they write my mother that I'm wounded? It'll be an awful shock to her. She won't know that I'm OK. You know how mothers are: tell her I'm wounded and she'll think I'm dead!" "Could you let Dad know instead of Mother. He can break it to her."

A bunch of men from D Company want to know if I have heard anything about their company commander, Lieutenant O. "He was right there with us all the time and he got hit. Do you know how he made out?" So I tell them, because I must, that I buried him. They want to know the truth, and there's no point in trying to fool them. Four of them lie there, and one sits on the edge of his bed. Tears stream from the eyes of some. The man on the bed sits, swearing softly and fluently. Their own wounds are forgotten. They compose an epitaph for a good officer and a brave man. "He was a swell guy!"

Stroup then related an incident that his mother—who still on occasion felt sensations from her amputated left leg—would have found particularly poignant.

One blond boy calls to me, "Chaplain, my right foot bothers me. I think it would help if you put something under it. Will you do it for me? I can't reach it." Of course I will, and I lift the blanket and there's no foot there. So I "put something under it" and fold the blanket back. "Does that feel better, Soldier?" He smiles up at me. "Yeah, that's a lot better. Thanks, Chaplain."

A long bronzed man speaks softly. "Chaplain, would you light a cigarette for me, please?" And he holds up the bandaged stump of his right arm in explanation. I put the cigarette between his lips, and he draws in deeply while his eyes look off into space as though he saw away down the future to life back home without a right hand. . . .

One boy is dying and his only thought is for his wife at home expecting a child in August. He wants to make sure that the news of his death won't get to her directly, but through someone else. I promise him that we'll get the news to his family instead. They can tell her, if they can, as they can.

There are surprisingly few shock cases considering what the men have been through. Some have been cut off, surrounded by Japanese. Some of them have endured hours of mortar fire. Some have had the enemy infiltrate into their camps at night and bayonet men in their "beds." But somehow their minds have withstood the shock, with the exception of a few.

There was one colored boy whom I had to be with a lot as I was the only one who could quiet him. But in that connection don't let anyone tell you that the colored boys are cowards. We don't have them in combat troops, but we do have them driving trucks and ducks, and they have gone through hell to take men and supplies in and bring wounded out, or evacuate men cut off by the enemy. Only one has cracked up. The rest have been cool, calm, and collected as they have worked day and night lifting, carrying, driving their trucks and driving themselves. . . .

I do what I can. There is water to carry to thirsty men, men to ease if possible on hard beds without pillows, men to feed who can't feed themselves, bedpans to be brought and emptied, and on and on. Mostly I spend my time talking to them personally and in groups trying my best to keep their minds occupied and their spirits high. It is little compared to what they deserve or need—or compared to what they are doing themselves! I saw one man with his head bandaged and his left arm and shoulder in a splint, feeding the boy next to him on a cot who hadn't the strength to feed himself. There was one man with a shrapnel wound in his head who held his end of the ward in constant mirth and did wonders to keep the spirits high. I told him how God must bless him for it, and he said, to return the compliment, "There just ain't words to tell you what you've meant to us." A gross exaggeration, but after he said it I wasn't tired anymore.

When I said good-bye to a shipload that we were evacuating, and they tried to express their thanks, I thanked God—looking into their brave smiling faces—that He had given me a chance to serve them. I hope all of us will prove ourselves worthy of their sacrifice. But I must close now. There has been a lull, but the work will begin again soon. Love to all,

Russell

It was unusual for Stroup to address his sister, my mother, in the family letter. The salutation on the following, written the very next day, suggests to me how much he needed to share the burdens of his heart.

Friday, June 2, 1944

Dearest Mother and Cranston (and Margretta
if you can get this to her),

Much of my time the past few days has been spent in a little field of white crosses beside the sea where the rows of graves have been growing as the bitter harvest is reaped. Most of the burials have fallen to me and a Catholic chaplain in a nearby unit. It's a heartbreaking business. It would be hard at home to have as many funerals every day, but out here where men are killed in the tragedy of combat, and placed in graves so very far from home, it becomes almost more than one can bear. The bodies are brought in on litters tenderly wrapped in blankets; sometimes carried by details, sometimes carried by their dearest friends. (There was one boy I found driving up and down the road searching for the cemetery with his best friend, dead in the jeep with him. He drove like a man who was drunk, for the tears blinded his eyes.) It is my task to gather from the dead their personal effects so that these may be sent home to their dear ones. I reverently remove precious letters kept to be read again and again, photographs of mothers, wives, and sweethearts, or perhaps baby pictures of those who are their immortality. It is not an easy thing to hold in your hand the smiling picture of a sweet-faced mother, knowing that soon the word will come to her which above all she dreads to hear. Of course I shall write to them all eventually telling them what I can of their boys. I hope when I come home that I may visit many of them. I think it would help.

But that would be hard for they are from everywhere: there is a young lieutenant from East Cleveland, a doctor from New York City, a Sergeant from Evansville, Indiana, a boy from Portland, Oregon, a lad from Memphis, Tennessee. Most of them have their religious preference indicated on their identification discs—whether Catholic, Protestant, or Jewish—and we bury them with appropriate rites. Where there is a doubt we have two services, both Catholic and Protestant.

There is a fine group of men in the Graves Registration Unit that cares for the bodies and digs the graves. They do their job so reverently. Always they stand by the grave, as we read the service, with bowed heads; or come to attention as we salute a soldier, dead.

Most of the graves are marked by white crosses, but there is the Star of David as well. I wish some of the anti-Semites at home could see them. I wish that they could know that their security and liberty have been bought for them at the price of the Jewish blood they despise. I would like to force them to stand with me at the grave of a Jewish doctor who in spite of wounds continued to minister to the needs of his boys, Gentile and Jew, until he died. I remember hearing some who bitterly resented the fact that Jews were crowding the medical profession. Well, there are plenty of boys out here who thank God fervently for Jewish doctors. For the Jews, I can read the great Psalms of comfort and assurance that are part of their wonderful gift to us all, and pray that the God of Abraham, Isaac, and Jacob will receive them unto Himself.

It is a good thing to know that our government shows such rare concern for our dead. Everything is done that can be done under the circumstances to accord them the tender attention and respect that is their due. We had no sooner landed than a spot of beauty had been chosen for the cemetery. There, with great care, the rows of graves were laid off. There the crosses and stars were placed. There, always in attendance, are those who receive and care for the bodies and call the chaplain to perform the last rites. You say that this is only right, and that is true, but in the life-and-death business of combat it is not easy. It shows a splendid spirit of reverence for human personality that refuses to treat carelessly these vacant temples of the Holy Spirit. I have felt that, as I assisted in this work, it is one of the hardest but finest things that I can do.

There are some exciting incidents. The first service I had—the benediction had just been pronounced when over the hill came a flight of enemy planes bombing and strafing the area where we were. I dived for a nearby shell hole, which seemed a mile across as I lay there watching the planes zooming toward me with guns blazing. In fact it seemed so very exposed—although it probably was safe enough—that when the first wave had passed I scurried to another and I hoped better hole, only to find that I had landed in a trench filled with ammunition. Fortunately nothing landed near enough to set it off.

Another time, as I stood with the lieutenant of the Graves Registration and the burial detail, a plane came over suddenly. Dropping my prayer book I dived for an open and vacant grave, landing with a thud on the bottom. The lieutenant, less alert than I, dove for the same grave and landed on top of me, and a third man on top of him. So we lay three deep—I feeling most comfortable with the two men between me and the sky, and the comforting walls of dirt around me. I had never thought that I would feel so fortunate to be in a grave. . . .

Upon occasion, although not often, I have helped to dig graves. Many times I have assisted in caring for the bodies, and as often as I could I have helped to lower them into the graves, or to carry them to the grave, because I like to do that service for such men. It is a proud privilege. I am an honored pallbearer, as well as priest.

It isn't often possible for the men from the outfit to be at their comrade's funeral, but it is interesting to see how the men in units near the cemetery come over and pay their respects by their presence. I was having one burial in the pouring rain and was all by myself, or so I thought, until I looked up and there was a lad from an AAA [anti-aircraft] outfit who had left his shelter and was standing at the foot of the grave, bare head dripping with rain. He had apparently seen me there alone and came over. After the benediction I turned and thanked him and he replied, "That's nothing, Chaplain, I wanted to be here."

A pathetic sight is the men who come into the cemetery and pass among the crosses looking for the names of men they may know and, when they find a name, stand there for a moment looking down, and then pass on.

But enough of death, or rather of burials . . . I've mentioned air raids and I might add that the AAA has been doing a grand job. I had somehow the idea that all anti-aircraft fire did was to keep planes high, but here the Japanese have been flying in low regardless. Night and day we spot them and hit them, and it's the exceptional plane that gets away. When we start firing it is certainly a sight and sound. At night the sky is literally laced with red streams of incendiaries streaking through the night in brilliant crisscross patterns. I have seen ack-ack fire before, but never to this extent. The air above us is literally filled with flying lead. I think that before long Tojo is going to get discouraged with the whole proposition and stay home. I won't be sorry for I hate to get nicely settled in bed only to climb out and into a hole. There are ten of us sleeping in an old Japanese chapel made of palm branches, and in the rear a long slit trench. It's amusing to see ten figures leap out of their respective hammocks and go streaking for the trench, tumbling in with great dispatch.

It was impossible last Sunday, since we landed on Saturday, to hold services, but this Sunday we will have them—although I don't know just where. I'm not at the moment attached to any particular unit and will hold them wherever they are needed in units that have no chaplains. I did attempt to hold two services this week, but one was rained out and the other scared out by a raid—so the score is zero so far. I'm not counting the informal services in the wards at the hospital. . . .

Just this moment you would hardly think a war was in progress for there isn't a sound except passing trucks and I can look out to a calm blue sea. I just realized this. I think it is the first time for a long time that there hasn't been noisy, constant fire. So in this quiet moment I'll close the letter sending you my dearest love and the assurance that all is well with me and will continue to be if I keep right on, as I intend to, taking excellent care of myself.

Russell

Saturday, June 3, 1944

Dear Folks,

Things continue about as they have been and there is little new that I can write. . . . There is a striking contrast between the American and the Japanese armies. The Japanese when they move into an area change the general features as little as possible. You would hardly know that they had installed thousands of men in a certain section. Using native labor they put up native houses for their troops. Installations are tucked away among the trees, difficult to find and blending into the landscape. The roads are improved only enough to get their vehicles over. Viewing a section from the air or from the sea you would think it was an untouched island where none but natives lived.

It is quite the contrary with the American army. When we move in we begin at once to transform the whole setting. Roads are built, tents and storage sheds go up, wires are strung, trees are cut down, hills are leveled off, docks are constructed, and in a few days the whole face of things is altered. There could never be any question that the Americans have moved in. We had heavy bulldozers, steam shovels, etc., working within four hours of our initial landing. It seems a distinct Anglo-Saxon trait. I am reminded how little the face of our continent was altered by the presence of the Indians and how even our first settlers transformed the terrain.

My personal engineering accomplishment consists of a very fancy air-raid shelter which, with Chaplain Graves, I have constructed. We first cut a pretty deep trench in the sand and decomposed coral. Over this we placed on rafters some corrugated iron roofing we picked up. On top of that we put palm tree logs. We covered the whole with a generous layer of sand. It would, we feel certain, be quite safe against anything but a direct hit, and it certainly has proved so thus far. . . .

Well, this is about the end of the page and the end of the news from somewhere in New Guinea for the present. I hope I can get it mailed. Much love as always,

Russell

Monday, June 5, 1944

Dearest Mother and Cranston,

Today, after so long a time, a little mail trickled in. . . . In the letters I was delighted to know of the visit of Margretta and Richard and so much about Richard and his development. . . .

Stroup received in the same mail a letter from my father, Allan Austin, then serving in Italy with the Fifth Army. He was the same age as Stroup and was also a captain. Assigned to an Allied Military Government unit, he moved north well behind the advancing combat lines to assist in the rebuilding of infrastructure and industry in liberated regions.

Allan's letter was very nice and I enjoyed it. He writes well. I feel guilty that I have not written to him. . . . How little actually he and many others will know of the war no matter how long they are in it. What we have been through here the past eight days is simply in another world altogether. To see enemy troops not a hundred yards from you and to be fired on by them; to crouch in a foxhole with mortar fire falling around you; to see an airplane with blazing machine guns diving, it seems, straight at you and to hear the bullets smacking into the trees above you; to carry in the bloody and burdened litters with their suffering cargo; to read the service over the open graves of fallen men; to count the gaping gashes made by enemy bayonets in American boys; to witness all the hideousness and heroism of war as it is at its worst is something that he will never know, thank God, and yet in a way it would be good for him and all others to see these things.

I have been fortunate, if one can call it that, to get here (as I did not in the last campaign) for all phases of war. I cannot write you of them now but will sometime. . . . The division to which I am attached has made quite a reputation for itself in various actions out here, and the men are seasoned jungle fighters. They have gained the particular animosity of the Japanese, which might be considered a testimony to their ability—there is hardly a broadcast from Tokyo that does not send some bitter message to our men, which is different from the rather friendly tone they assume for most of the American boys in the Southwest Pacific. I think that they have done their share and should have a rest from it all. Maybe after this operation is completed they will get it, but then I shall probably be with some other outfit.

It is three o'clock on a Monday afternoon and I am trying to write this from the hospital. I got no sleep to speak of last night and until this moment I have been busy in the wards, but we have just finished evacuating a lot of patients by ship and, after going around to distribute cigarettes, candy, and chewing gum to those who remain, I'm taking a little time off.

The guns are firing fiercely just at the moment—both our artillery and the navy guns offshore. You can hear the report of the guns going off and the sound of the shells as they pass overhead and then, after a few seconds, the detonation as of giant casks bumping down stairs as they land among the enemy. It is a comforting feeling to realize that they are going in the right direction. . . .

Had a good service yesterday. Had planned three but due to circumstances over which I had no control I only got through one. But at that I did better than most chaplains here. It was good to have your letters. I return with interest all the love you expressed in them. All is well.

Russell

Cranston had asked his brother to send home a captured gun, a Japanese flag, and other souvenirs. Although Cranston was older than his brother, his illness seemed to keep alive an adolescent fascination with the equipment of war. Stroup wrote a letter addressing Cranston's particular interests, experimenting with the one-page, photo-condensed V-Mail that constricted his writing but usually reached its destination more swiftly.

Cranston Stroup [V-Mail heading]

I have written very few V Mail but will try one now just to see how it gets through to you. Yours certainly come best that way but I usually have so much to say that it restricts me in my expression. I was so glad to get your letter of May 5th, just one month after it was written. . . .

I think I can say with assurance that even you, with your love of guns, would get enough of them out here. I am in a hospital at the moment . . . and yet I can look around me and see carbines, Gerrands, tommy guns, etc. They lie about in great profusion and they are used too—although not in the hospital of course. There have been some patients, however, who insisted on keeping their arms near them, so accustomed have they become to sleeping with rifle beside them.

As I write our artillery and naval guns are pouring a tremendous barrage into the Japanese positions. You would think to hear it that no one could endure such withering fire, but the strange thing is that they do. After it is all over and our infantry advance they will find plenty of live opposition. This island is honeycombed with limestone and coral caves where it is possible to hole up in comparative safety and wait for the firing to cease. That is the enemy strategy. . . . His one big advantage is the terrain in which he fights, which is all in favor of those who are on the defensive.

I doubt if anywhere out here or even in Europe have the AAA boys shown up as well as they have here. They have taken a tremendous toll of the planes which have come over. I have seen a lot come down in flames at night as well as in the daytime. I was amused day before yesterday, peeking out of a foxhole, to see one of the anti-aircraft boys take his seat before his multiple set of fifty-caliber machine guns, spit on his hands, rub them together, and then take a grip on the handles with a most beatific expression on his face and turn a withering fire on a Jap plane that came down the beach dropping its load of bombs.

The hospital kitchen is the one place where they bake fresh bread, and the cook promised the ack-ack boys near the hospital a loaf of fresh bread for every plane they brought down. He now says he will have to go back on his promise if they keep knocking them down at the present rate. . . .

There are a lot of things I might write of, for instance the boy going out on a litter today, being evacuated to the rear by ship. Beside him on the litter was a Jap saber and across his head was a deep gash that same saber had made. But he got the officer and the saber and seemed filled with a vast content. So am I at the moment, thinking of you and sending my deepest love.

Russell

Wednesday, June 7, 1944

Dearest family,

The bald statement that American troops had landed in France reached us yesterday and, while we are eagerly awaiting further details, we are quite absorbed by the simple fact itself. Engrossed as we well might be with our own action we still are very excited. I go to each ward in the morning and give them a summary of the world news and the local rumors—as I get them at division headquarters—and I find a most appreciative audience. I told them this morning that their families at home will have to look back among the ads to find any news of our operations now that things have opened up in Western Europe. . . .

The reaction of the men is, of course, that the landing will do much to shorten the war and so benefit us as well as the rest. Characteristically, they discuss how much tougher it is going to be for the invasion forces than it is for us since they are fighting the Germans. What they don't take into consideration is the fact that we have a lot more men and supplies in Europe to fight with and certainly don't have the difficult terrain that we must combat here. I still say that the toughest theater of war is here—but that's natural since I'm here and prejudiced. I surely don't want to imagine anything tougher!

. . . There was an Australian war correspondent here who said that he had been in at Guadalcanal and that it was a picnic compared to this. We won't get the same publicity as that action, however, since it was one of the first and also the Marines were in on it and they always get the write-ups. I suppose that we can anticipate that things will get more difficult as we get closer to the Philippines or to the inner perimeter of Japanese defenses. We seem to have arrived at the edge of that now. . . .

Russell

Sunday, June 11, 1944

Dearest family,

This is Sunday and I have had a busy morning. I got down to the hospital early and made my rounds of the wards distributing news, tobacco, and good cheer. I had to hurry because I had a service at 10 o'clock. It was held in a large tent made to hold thirty beds and was crowded with men seated and standing. Most of them were walking wounded and a fine audience they made. Fortunately nothing disturbed the service. . . .

The boys in the wards are always talking of home and comparing the merits of their several states, as they lie on their litters in the wards. Such a discussion was in progress and a lad with a bandaged head raised himself on his elbow and drawled: "Wall, there's one thing Arkansas has got that no other state has." Someone fired back, "What the H— could Arkansas have that no other state has?" To which the boy replied: "MY HOME!"

One man from Georgia, a long lean tobacco chewing Cracker, asked me to write a letter for him, volunteering the information. "I wish you'd write a letter to my wife cause I reckon it'll be a spell before I'm able." Then he added, to orient me, I guess: "She's a good Christian woman. Course she's a might difficult to get along with sometimes but I 'spect I could overlook that if I was with her now."

Another favorite topic of conversation is what you are going to do after the war. This was going full blast in one ward. I turned to a silent fellow who had been contributing nothing to the conversation. "What are you going to do?" I inquired. "I kind of figure I'll return to my first love." "What's that?" "C—y—ow—es"—which is the best I can do to suggest his pronunciation of "Cows." "There's the Ryder outfit up north of Gardiner and I kin go back there any time I'm a mind to, get seventy dollars a month too, seein' as how I've got my own string of horses. That is I did have if they ain't all dead before this thing is over." . . .

There are tragedies too that should be remembered. One boy sat with his head buried in his hands. He wanted nothing that I could bring to him, nor would he answer me but only shook his head. I tried my best to interest him in something but without avail. Finally I got his story. He had been wounded by a shell that killed two of his companions: boys he had known all his life, boys who lived in the same block, the comrades of his childhood, his schoolmates, boys with whom he had shared dates and all the intimacies of adolescence, boys whose families he knew and to whom he must return, the Jonathans to his David whom he loved with a "love passing the love of women."

What could I say to assuage the grief of a loss so overwhelming? I think that God gave me the right word. "Son," I said, "I know you've been cruelly hurt. There isn't anything I can say to comfort you, but the ward here is filled with boys who have gone through so much. They need cheering just as you do and it doesn't help them to see you sitting here like this. I don't ask you to forget what you've been through, but I do ask that you try to hide your feelings for their sake." When next I came through the ward he was feeding the lad in the litter next to his.

The recommendation to hide feelings is characteristic of Stroup's stoicism. While Stroup did persuade the man to tell his story, the advice he gave is surely different from modern therapy for grief or shock, which would encourage continued expression. Yet a field hospital on the front lines was no setting for psychotherapy. It was a dangerous, high-stress location, and Stroup asked patients to bear their situation with as much cheer as they could muster in the hope, perhaps, of more thorough treatment following evacuation to a nearby hospital ship. They all lived, day after day, in a situation that did not permit thorough healing.

A boy came to me yesterday. He had been to the cemetery to find his brother's grave and had inquired there who had buried him. He then went to the trouble to find me and thank me for doing what I could for his brother. "Mother would want me to thank you, I know," he said. He seemed so lost away out here with his brother dead and his family so far away. My heart went out to him. . . .

There is a look in the faces of men who have borne the brunt of battle like nothing that I have ever seen. But I shall never forget it as long as I live. Gaunt and drawn by fatigue and suffering, they stare straight ahead with the horror of men who have looked through the gates of hell. Of course, that is only when you catch them unawares. Their great concern is to hide their suffering and meet life with a smile. There is nothing quite so sad as pain that twists itself into a grin. Yet, while the scars are there and the ache in the heart is like a remembered wound, life does go on. Somehow they are permitted to forget enough to live once more. God has a way of healing our hurts with time.

While I have dwelt largely on my own experiences I would not want you to think that I have been unique or even that I have been through half as much as other chaplains here. There are the ones who came in with infantry regiments and stayed with them from the beginning, who have not been away from the front for a moment since they arrived. Several of them have been almost constantly under fire and have acquitted themselves gallantly. A couple, especially, will probably be decorated for their bravery and the inspiration and help they have been to their men. As one infantry captain put it, "There wasn't any of us that showed the guts that Chaplain did. If he had the slightest fear he never showed it." Their part was much harder than mine, so far as constant danger is concerned, and to them I take off my hat and stand at attention. As the book of Judges has it, "These are they who jeopardized their lives in the high places of the field."

My own experiences at the front have been spasmodic, and while there is no safe place here, by comparison I have been safe. I feel quite inadequate as I compare their contribution with mine but console myself with the thought that I have done what I could. I suppose that actually I have been able to do as much good, but at much less risk to myself. While I have been willing to go forward and stay there, the division headquarters seems to feel that my place is here, perhaps out of respect for my age or perhaps because I am not really a member of the organization. I have never felt less fit than younger men, but they may be right in feeling that the front is for youth. I suppose I must content myself with "staying by the stuff."

Well, soon I must go back to my charges for my afternoon call with candy and chewing gum. A special greeting to Mother on Father's Day. You have been both to me.

Russell

Responding to the stalemate of the first few days, Command ordered a third battalion to Biak, the 163d Infantry. Stroup had manifested a competitive desire, not just to give of himself, but to give more than anyone. Now he resolved his feelings of inadequacy by securing an assignment with the most forward unit of these reinforcements, a group of seasoned jungle fighters. On June 12, as part of a plan to clear the major Japanese pocket of resistance that overlooked the principal airport and prevented its use, Company L moved along the high coral ridges to seize Hill 320, which overlooked the Japanese installations to the south as well as—they would discover later—a ravine to the north containing many large caves used by the Japanese for storing supplies and for refuge from attack. This isolated position could not have been defended had the Japanese chosen to expel the company, but they were focused on the larger army units moving toward them across the airfield below.

Commanders visited Hill 320 in the days ahead to observe the battle. From that base Company L reconnoitered miles of surrounding countryside, identifying Japanese positions from the rear. Later, as naval and shore

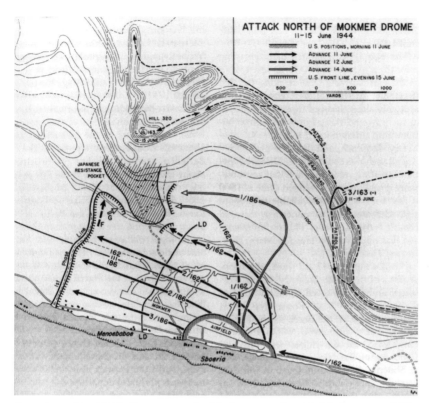

ATTACK NORTH OF MOKMER DROME
11-15 June 1944

U.S. POSITIONS, MORNING 11 JUNE
ADVANCE 11 JUNE
ADVANCE 12 JUNE
ADVANCE 14 JUNE
U.S. FRONT LINE, EVENING 15 JUNE

From June 12, 1944, Stroup served with Company L, 163d Infantry, on Hill 320, overlooking the Japanese resistance pocket. The road where he encountered an ambush probably followed the hatch lines toward the lower right corner of the map. From Smith, Approach to the Philippines, *333.*

artillery assaults and infantry advances increased pressure on the Japanese resistance pocket, Company L, with reinforcements, intercepted the retreating enemy. Here, for twelve days, until the company was relieved, Stroup served in the midst of the most brutal and difficult warfare of the Pacific campaign.

Friday, June 16, 1944

Dearest family,

Just after writing to you about the comparative quiet of my assignment to the hospital, I got shifted to a front-line unit and am at present serving with them at an advanced post. I doubt if I shall be here long, but for the present it is rather rugged going, not so much from the point of view of danger as the rough life which is necessary. . . . I'm not out with the patrols that really take it from the enemy. We do have some enemy infiltration; a group came through the other night and left two of their number behind them less than fifty yards from where I was sleeping, when the outposts drove them off—as they always do. . . .

Russell

From June 20 onward the fighting was particularly brutal as the Japanese were pushed back into the caves north of Hill 320. They would not surrender, would not retreat, and would not quit fighting. Stroup's unit, along with others, was ordered to clean out the caves. He was not so thoughtless as to write home about this aspect of the battle, but after he returned he told stories in my hearing that sounded like this official history of June 20: "From a multitude of crevices and cracks around the caves, and from the interior of the sump holes themselves, came a great deal of rifle and light automatic weapons fire, an the battalion was unable to get any men down into the sump depressions. Drums of gasoline were rolled into many caves and then ignited in the hope that most of the Japanese would be killed. But the enemy fire continued almost unabated" (Smith, Approach to the Philippines, *373). Stroup confined his next letter to the lighter side.*

Thursday, June 22, 1944

Dear Cranston,

I am with a grand group of men—much like the old 100th as far as officers are concerned, but the men are a rugged bunch coming mostly from Montana, Idaho, and the Northwest generally. They have had plenty of battle experience and are one of the two best jungle-fighting outfits in the Southwest Pacific.

You realize the difference when you are with them. There is none of the indiscriminate firing of weapons that made life perilous in the other campaign. If they fire a shot you know there's a Jap there, and usually a dead one. You have a feeling of confidence when you are with them, which is very soothing. . . .

The other night our artillery was dropping a barrage around our ears, as sometimes happens when you are as close to the Japs as we are, and the air was filled with shrapnel. The major telephoned the artillery and in a bored southern drawl acquainted them with the facts. They inquired whether there were any casualties. He replied, "No, you all aren't hitting anything, but you surely are annoyin' the boys." The firing stopped. . . .

This is truly difficult country to fight in. There is a myriad of steep, rough, rocky coral ridges covered with a dense forest you have to cut your way through. It takes hours to travel a few hundred yards. . . . Where the other units are fighting the country is fairly clear, but we have been given the hard job of holding a large piece of territory toward which the other troops are driving the Japs. We are supposed to catch them as they come out. The trouble is that since we only have so many, they sometimes reverse the process. The country is ideal for ambushes, and there is no possible way to discover the ambushers. You just have to go on and hope that when the Japs reveal themselves by firing, they won't do too much damage. Some of the fighting is the fiercest sort of hand-to-hand business with automatics, knives, and bare hands. It is very rough going with very determined opposition. Anytime you move beyond the perimeter you run the risk of finding Japs. When we go from here to the regimental headquarters, as I often have to do, you are pretty likely to run into some. You urge me to remember my infantry training, and I'm not likely to forget it.

My work has been much appreciated. The C.O. has requested that I be assigned to them permanently as I'm "the best —— Chaplain" they ever had. . . .

Don't worry. I shall be taking swell care of myself. Loads of love,

Russell

At home Cranston, proud of his brother, took delight in repeating the phrase "Best God-damned Chaplain," to the annoyance of his mother.

Two days after the previous letter, when his unit was withdrawing from the front for rest and he was safely out of danger, Stroup could tell a story of heroism without, he hoped, worrying his family unduly.

Saturday, June 24, 1944

Dearest family,

There is a road that leads from our forward position where I am stationed to the regimental headquarters in the rear. The miles it wanders uphill and down lie through a brushy country made to order for ambuscades. While we control the important points, there are long stretches where parties of Japanese wander and, as occasion offers, waylay our men.

UNITED STATES ARMY

June 24th, 1944.

Dearest Family,

There is a road that leads from our forward position where I am stationed to the Reg. Hqrs in the rear. The miles it wanders up hill and down lies through a brushy country made to order for ambuscades. While we control the important points there are long stretches where parties of Japanese wander and as occasion offers waylay our men. The other day, I started down this perilous road carrying a body to the rear for burial. I was in a truck with what seemed to be an adequate guard — the driver in the front with me and three men in the body of the truck with the body. Of course all but myself were armed. We stopped at K. to on the way where a wounded man had just been brought in. I saw him and then went on. He was to follow later in an ambulance. There was also a car load of high ranking officers who were in a tour of inspection and I paid my respects to them. They, too, were following us after a while.

About three miles below we came over a rise in the road and over the other side saw a terrifying sight. To the left of the road stood a Jeep — a soldier was slumped forward in the front seat and another lay crumpled in the rear — apparently the section of an ambush. I called for the driver to stop but he traveled about fifty yards before he could. Opposite us on the right side lay two more men, apparently dead. As we ground to a stop one man raised himself on his elbow and feebly waved his hand — I thought it a signal of distress. But then I heard him call "Japs!! Keep going!" I called out "Where?" and he pointed over his shoulder and replied "Eight or ten, that way." By now one of my men, a German named Herman who used to be in the Nazi army, called "I'm going to get him, who's going with me?" I said "Wait a minute and we'll all go." I wanted to size up the situation first altho it was pretty obvious and not very encouraging. We could see that the Japs had already destroyed a force equal to ours and by the warning of the wounded man there were still eight or ten Japs, double our number, in the vicinity

Stroup was temporarily separated from his typewriter when he composed the only letter in the entire collection written on United States Army stationery.

The other day I started down this perilous road carrying a body to the rear for burial. I was in a truck with what seemed to be an adequate guard—the driver in the front with me and three men in the back of the truck with the body. Of course, all but myself were armed. We stopped at K Company on the way, where a wounded man had just been brought in. I spoke to him and went on; he was to follow later in an ambulance. We met a carload of high-ranking officers who were on a tour of inspection, and I paid my respects to them. They, too, were to follow us after a while.

About three miles further we came over a rise in the road and, on the other side, saw a terrifying sight. To the left of the road stood a jeep: a soldier was slumped forward in the front seat and another lay crumpled in the rear, apparently the victims of an ambush. I called for the driver to stop, but he traveled about fifty yards before he could. There, opposite us on the right side, lay two more men, apparently dead. However, as we ground to a stop one man raised himself on his elbow and feebly waved his hand. I thought it was a signal of distress. But then I heard him call, "Japs!! Keep going!" I called out, "Where?" and he pointed over his shoulder and replied, "Eight or ten, that way."

By now one of my men, a German named Herman who used to be in the Nazi army, called, "I'm going to get him. Who's going with me?" I said, "Wait a minute, and we'll all go." I wanted to size up the situation first, although it was pretty obvious and not very encouraging. We could see that the Japs had already destroyed a force equal to ours, and by the warning of the wounded man there were still eight or ten Japs, double our number, in the vicinity. Frankly, I was plenty frightened. It seemed like certain death to stop. My head said, "Let's get out of here." But somehow my heart wouldn't let me. I will confess that it was far from easy to get out of the cab and into the open where the wounded man was. In that terrible moment I tested myself. I had often wondered what I would do, and now I had to decide.

Of course, there was only one decision, and once I had made it and gotten out of that lovely protected cab, I never again felt the slightest hesitation or for that matter, oddly enough, the slightest fear. I ordered three of the men with guns to stand ready facing the direction we thought the Japs were in, and another man to follow me. All of this took less time than it does for me to tell it. We reached the wounded man and lifted him up and carried him back to the truck, where we placed him on the litter from which we removed the body that had been there. When we reached him he had said, "Don't stay for me. Get the h—l out of here. I'm finished anyhow." He was willing to stay there and die rather than put us in peril. In fact he seemed quite annoyed that we wouldn't do what he said.

After we had gotten him to safety, I went back to the man he had been lying near, to see if he were alive. He wasn't. Then, although I felt certain that the men in the jeep were dead, I had two of my men stay by the truck while two went with me the long, long 150 feet or so to the jeep. There I made certain they had died, and then wasted no time getting back to the truck and on our way.

In the truck I sat holding the wounded man because he wanted to sit up and I thought he would be comfortable leaning against me. I then began to worry about the ambulance and also the officers, coming after us—fearing that they would receive no warning. We drove fast because we wanted to get the wounded man to the hospital, because we wanted to warn the regimental headquarters to phone back and stop all vehicles, and because we were just plumb anxious to get out of there ourselves.

We had gone about two miles when we met a patrol, with an ambulance, coming out to the scene of the ambuscade. We learned that two vehicles, unknown to us, had passed by the ambush scene, refused to face the peril of stopping, but reached the regiment to warn them and get a patrol on the way. We transferred the wounded man to the ambulance and went on to headquarters. The patrol continued to the scene of the ambush where they encountered the Japs. They killed two Japanese, but the rest escaped. Why—since clearly they were still there—the Japs didn't fire on us, I will never know. Perhaps it was the Providential care of which I am constantly conscious. Obviously it wasn't because of the pitiful force we had.

The courage of my men was superb. Even if I had ordered them not to stop, I think they would have insisted on it, although they knew the odds against them. As for the wounded man, his anxiety for our safety was beyond praise. They had been ambushed, two of his companions were killed at once, he and the third had run for the cover they never reached as the Japs dropped them with fire on the way. He had then seen the Japs shoot again, bayonet the three dead men, and then start for him. He played dead, so they shot him and passed on. That he could be willing, after such a terrifying experience, to stay there and die so we might be safe, that was as brave a thing as I have ever heard of.

At my recommendation the command is considering awarding him a medal—posthumously, as the poor lad died the next day. He had seven wounds.

As a matter of fact we might all be awarded one—the general commended me verbally—if it were not for the technicality that we were not under fire! That, I think, detracts nothing from the courage of the men since they had every reason to believe that they were walking into a dangerous situation. However, we are not interested in medals. I know we receive the Order of the Good Samaritan since we refused to pass by on the other side as two other groups had done, but stopped and brought in the man from the Jericho road.

I told you I wouldn't walk into danger and I won't, but sometimes danger comes to you and there is nothing you can do but face it and see it through. I wonder if the original Good Samaritan was as scared as I was before I went over to give aid. That is something the Bible commentaries have missed. Sometime I might write a book on biblical experiences in wartime. . . .

Right now I'm reliving the plague of flies that harassed the Egyptians. It is worse than the Japanese. Only nighttime brings relief. I wish you hadn't trained me to dislike flies, Mother, then I might be more accepting. But I'm doing all right, and this business will soon be over. The worst is over now. Love to all.

Russell

Stroup's bravery may have had an immediate impact on his religious ministry with the troops. He certainly expressed a close identification with them.

Thursday, June 29, 1944

Dearest family,

Fortunately we have been in reserve for the past few days. . . . I had a splendid service here on Sunday, the first time I had a chance to get any large part of my men together, and an even more gratifying service last night when I had almost a hundred men for a midweek service, which is quite unusual. These boys have been mighty responsive and I seem in a short time to have made a place for myself, even though it may not be for long. . . .

I spent the other night down on the beach with the [Engineer] Group, the first I have been with them for a long time. They were mighty glad to see me. Even though they are far to the rear I spent a more uneasy night than I have at the front, for we had a couple of mean air raids. Up here, at least, we don't get those. The air raids are more terrifying than ground attacks. They may continue after other opposition is broken up. So I have returned to the "safety" of the front lines, or near them. I have certainly seen this particular war from all angles.

Just before my previous campaign ended I had a slight attack of bronchitis, or something like it. Now I'm annoyed with the same thing again, near the end of this one. I hope to conquer it, or to wear it out. . . .

I'm thinking of the fact that in a couple of days it will be Cranston's birthday, wishing that I could be with him on that day; or any day! Love,

Russell

Stroup was restless when he could not be fully useful to those in combat or to those suffering its consequences. Yet during his time on Hill 320 he began initiatives to limit his period in combat. In his letter of June 16, he discussed the desirability of leaving the service after a year on active duty, suggesting the Lynchburg congregation could petition the Chaplain's Corps for his return. "I am not eager to spend my life in the army. I am anxious to do my part out here but no more than that."

Stroup returned from Hill 320 exhausted, both physically and spiritually. His dreams of returning home intensified.

Sunday, July 2, 1944

Dearest Cranston,

Both because I got a grand letter from you yesterday and because it is your birthday, I want to write even though this is a busy Sunday. I did want to get a Jap flag home to you for your birthday but I couldn't send it out after our last "show" and I haven't been able to send it out from here. . . .

With your usual acuteness, your prognostication is quite correct regarding the location of the campaigns, but you did miss the original location, which gives you only 66 2/3 percent. Better luck next time. . . .

A letter from Margretta tells me that her army general friend in Washington is a good friend of General Arnold of the Chaplain's

Corps. I think he should be able to get me a nice cushy job in Washington in the chief of chaplain's office where I would have plenty of leisure to write up my experiences and do some speech making, and get to see you all. What do you think of that for an idea? . . . I hope that by your next birthday I shall be with you again,

Russell

About this time Stroup did receive reassuring news from the Lynchburg church, which was making do with a retired pastor while he was on leave to serve in the army. Now that he had been absent for more than a year, he asked a confidant in the congregation, Joe Banks, whether it would be better for the church if he resigned his pastorate. In a letter to his mother he enclosed the reply.

With reference to your suggestion that it might be well for you to offer the Church your resignation. NO! You most assuredly should not do this! Man, you are one of us. The distance between you and your congregation, while considerable in miles, is nothing in mind and spirit and love and mutual interest. . . . Your church has, I think, buckled on the armor of faith a few notches tighter, and we feel a knit-togetherness not before so apparent. And, although Dr. Moffett is liked, well liked, and is one splendid man, and is filling in beautifully, still the congregation looks to you as Pastor. We think of you, talk of you, pray for you daily. You belong! Now do not forget this.

Tuesday, July 4, 1944

Dearest family,

I wonder if, nowadays, parents still make holidays so noteworthy for their children that when they grow older they will think of home more poignantly on such days than on any others?

Out here the Fourth is neither safe nor sane. . . . In this type of war you don't take Cherbourg and have the remaining Germans surrender. Here, even when the enemy opposition disintegrates, there continues a hunting and harrowing of the remainder until all are accounted for. As one Jap wrote in his diary, "We are determined to fight to the bitter end. To die is easy, but to live is difficult. I will not die until I kill one of the enemy." . . . Their courage is amazing. It is often blind, unreasonable, and reckless, yet dangerous. It is impossible to anticipate what they may do. . . .

I am glad that you have been able to know something of what I was doing and where, even though it may have caused concern. I may be wrong but I've gone on the supposition that, for you, to know is better than being uncertain. You and Cran are quite right in thinking that my infantry training, which was of the best, has stood me in good stead. . . .

Some men near me are playing cards with a set that has a cocker spaniel on the back like our dog General, and this makes me homesick, or perhaps I should say this increases it. I can close my eyes and see you all as you would be about this time of day, supper time, with General all eager for the meal to begin. He wouldn't be any more eager than I would be if I were there. I would give a thousand dollars to have one of Hazel's good meals again. Of course the men here talk a lot about the meals they have at home and I'm always telling them what a perfect cook we have. Hazel is becoming quite famous in the Southwest Pacific. . . .

What a grand thing it is that Margretta can see you as frequently as she does and that Richard can be there at fairly regular intervals. . . . I hate to miss these years of his that are so formative. There are many things I hate to miss. . . .

I had two grand services Sunday with two separated parts of my battalion. One was in the morning and one in the evening. Both majors have attended each service I have had after the first, which they did not attend—but I held it close enough to their tent, purposely, so that they couldn't help but hear, and that brought them out for the next one. It is, according to the other officers, the first time they have showed up at services. I heard them discussing the sermon later and telling a visitor about it. I also heard a lot of men going over it. They all seemed pleased. But they all have put up with some rather inferior stuff as far as sermons go.

The chaplains here, most of them, do a grand job in combat, but they don't have much to offer in other ways. They are consecrated and courageous but not too intelligent. That is not the most important thing but it does help. Of course they all make the mistake of trying to talk the men's language, and discuss the things they think the men are interested in, when the men really want to hear about God.

I went to some of our units that are on the front line on Sunday afternoon and, while we were too close to the enemy to hold services, I did get around and talked to the men and distributed some Testaments and some fairly decent tracts I had gotten hold of. I found a couple of boys on an outpost. They said, "Watch this, Chappie." One of them snaked around to the side of the hole with his Browning automatic rifle and peered over the top with the gun in position while the other cautiously lifted his helmet on a stick to the level of the foxhole. There was a sharp ping as a sniper let go at it, and the other lad opened up with the machine gun in the direction of the sound. "I don't think I got him," he remarked with some sorrow. They had been doing that off and on for two days. I asked them how far away the sniper was and they said they didn't know exactly, but that he could throw over hand grenades, and did, but that the grenades all went over their heads and landed in the deep hole that lay behind them where they exploded without harm. "We figure he can't possibly land them here," they said, but I wasn't so sure and after a whispered conversation I left. It was a strange part of a Sunday afternoon.

Russell

A letter from his mother gave Stroup more details of Margretta's efforts on his behalf to arrange a reassignment home. Deeply fatigued from the five-week Biak campaign, Stroup wrote a forceful response to insure that those efforts did not misfire. He did not want to exercise his prerogative of asking to be relieved from combat duty because he had passed his thirty-eighth birthday. Rather, he wanted to be called home.

Sunday, July 9, 1944

Dearest family,

. . . You mention Margretta talking to some general about me. She got it all wrong. I knew that only through the command out here could I get relieved from the army, if I wanted to under the thirty-eight-year-old provision. What I suggested, half in fun, was that she might be influential in getting me a nice soft job in the chief of chaplains' office in Washington where I could take it easy after a year of combat out here. The chief of chaplains can assign any chaplain to a job anywhere if he wishes, but he couldn't get them discharged under the thirty-eight-year-old provision. Seriously, I have the feeling that at my age a year out here is about all I could stand physically or spiritually. I've been here half that time already. If I am going to try to get back in another six months it is not too early to plan for it, only I'm not quite certain how I should go about it. It did occur to me that an interim step might be a job back in the States. I wouldn't like the work, but it would give me a chance to do some speaking and writing on the side, and that would have its compensations. I know it isn't easy to get into the office in Washington, but with the proper influence it might be managed . . . with discretion. I would not want others to know about it. . . .

Another possibility would be for my church to insist to the Defense Service Council that they need me back there. The Defense Service Council might prevail upon me to try for release under the thirty-eight-year-old provision; and prevail upon the chief of chaplains' office to persuade the general to grant me the release. He would, at their suggestion. In that way the impetus would come from the church and not from me, which would be better. . . .

It will not be easy if I go from combat to combat, as it looks as though I might. Really there is little else that one can do. I think a trip to Australia might help, for that would be something entirely different, but that isn't very possible. Just to "rest" for two or three months in New Guinea is in some ways worse than being in combat. You are always uncomfortable, and there is nothing to stimulate you except the work which in such intervals is not very arduous and often pretty dull. . . .

We had a fine service this morning. The major remarked that the men have never turned out before as they do since I came, and that the

number grows greater with every service. That's encouraging, especially as only recently have we had a chance to put on anything like a real service. I'll probably have another service this evening for the men who have been out on patrol today and couldn't get here this morning, and of course for any others who wish to come. It will be mostly singing. . . .

I'm feeling much better than I did last week and am almost myself again. A little more rest and less excitement and I'll be OK. I took one of the links out of the watch bracelet you sent me and I could take out another, but I won't as I hope to get back some of the lost weight.

Russell

PS: It won't be necessary to send this on to Margretta. I've written similarly to her.

Stroup wrote the following note to Cranston on the back of a Japanese postcard:

Wednesday, July 12, 1944

Here you have a very graphic and quite unartistic representation of the "ever invincible," as they say, Japanese army crawling to the attack.

Lately most of the crawling has been in the other direction and the Sons of Heaven seem to be on their way home. We are at the moment engaged in the somewhat tedious task of rooting out the remainder of the Japanese.

I however am back with the 1112th [Engineer Group] and so will not be in on any more of that sort of operation, which is reserved for the infantry. Just what my future plans will be I don't know. The battalion and division I have been with have both asked for my assignment—the division chaplain promising me a job as regimental chaplain if I come back to them. It is all up to the powers that be and I'll just sit tight and see what happens.

Russell

5

"What a Sense of Release
When I Go on Ship Board"

Stroup, delighted to leave Biak, conveyed the news with graceful images.
He shipped westward three hundred miles, part way toward Hollandia, to
Maffin Bay—a large staging area on the north coast of New Guinea from
which other invasions would soon be dispatched. There he would be close to
senior officers who might assist him.

Sunday, July 16, 1944

Dearest family,

You cannot know what a wonderful sense of release comes when I go
on ship board even for a short trip. It has always been so and the fascination lasts. Now especially, for there you find cleanliness and comfort
and order. I suppose a real sailor would scorn these strange LSTs as no
ship at all, and certainly for me there are better vessels, but it is still
the sea. Our voyage will be short, to some place of preparation and/or
organization, but I shall enjoy every moment of it. When we reach the
end, perhaps I can get the leave to Australia I'm working for. . . .

In combat time passes much more quickly than in the periods
of preparation in between, so perhaps I am lucky to have had such
uninterrupted combat experience. The last three months have gone by
much more rapidly than the first three.

The food on board is wonderful. Yesterday noon, our first meal,
we had chicken à la king, incredible, and *ice* tea. This morning for
breakfast, while we didn't have the eggs we were all hoping for, we
did get hot cakes with *honey*. . . . There was also real orange juice this
morning. And all of this served at a *table* by waiters who offer you their
platters! I could enjoy C-rations under such conditions. And most
heavenly of all, *not a single fly*. I've been eating at a rough board table

where we set a piece of bread and jam in the center in a vain attempt to attract the hoards of buzzing bluebottles away from our own food. This is the life!!

They even have books, a few dog-eared volumes. I sat down last night on a leather upholstered seat and read Conrad's "Chance" in one joyous sitting, even though I like that about the least of his efforts. He is at his worst when he tries to write about women. His females are the least alive of any creatures in fiction. . . .

Russell

When he reached Maffin Bay, Stroup learned that the 1112th Engineer Group would be reorganized as a construction command group to supervise other engineering units. There would be no place for chaplains or medics, so he would need to find another assignment. The 239th Combat Engineer Battalion asked for his services, as did the 41st Infantry Division he had just left. Stroup found the latter more appealing.

Wednesday, July 19, 1944

Dearest family,

. . . From the point of view of comfort and ease the first would be preferable, but somehow I can't bring myself to accept that. . . . In an infantry outfit there is more to be done whether in combat or in rest periods. . . . You can get closer to your men and you can do more for your men. . . . The engineers are always a member of some task force and their chaplain is usually, in the initial phase, asked to help out with the front-line troops, so you share their perils without being part of them. So I think I shall go to the 41st Division or, I should say, go back to the 41st. It really is a first-class outfit, one of the best, and I have enjoyed my work with them. There is another thought to consider. They have been out here longer than any other division, and if any division is to be sent home, they will be. . . .

We are just sitting around right now and if it were not for the rain, which is pretty constant, and the ants, I would be most comfortable. The flies, thank heaven, are very few. I guess we can put up with the ants. We are camped in a thick rain forest, so that accounts for the little fellows. The tide of battle passed by here some time since so everything is pretty quiet and you sleep at night. I'm with the [111 2th Engineer] Group, which is a very small bunch, but we have comfortable tents and pretty good food, and I have no complaints. . . .

Things look better and better in Europe. But even after our invasion of France we can't steal the spotlight from Russia. They keep on rolling along. If, as I believe, the Germans will do anything to prevent the Russians from getting into Germany, they will have to sue for peace pretty soon, for the Russians are knocking at the door. Having done so much to win the war in Europe the Russians can do even more to hasten the end in Asia if, after Hitler is defeated, they join us against Japan as I believe they will do. One thing is certain: they will then put themselves in a position to demand what they will in the postwar world. It is fortunate for us that they want little beyond peace, security, and a chance to develop their own tremendous country.

What stupendous problems we all face when the war is over. . . . Those of us who have been in the war itself may have an increased prestige, especially those also more mature. I hope to make my contribution then. Taking the men in the army as typical, I sometimes become very discouraged with the prospects. Too many of them can see no further than getting home, having a steak dinner, and either living with their wives or getting wives. They do not seem to grasp the bigger issues involved if all the people are to have steaks and homes. Of course too many have the point of view that if I can have my steak and home it is of no concern to me what others do not have.

Against this spirit I labor. There might be a different world tomorrow if all or even a large part of our chaplains were doing the same. We might not reach the majority but I doubt if the majority matters. Always they will live largely below the belt, their whole lives governed by those organs, with the heart and head useless appendages. . . .

Russell

Saturday, July 22, 1944

Dearest family,

. . . Most Americans refuse to believe that the Japanese are not essentially different from any other people. They know when they are licked and they will not fight to the bitter end, as a nation, when the fact finally dawns upon them. The common Jap soldier may, but Japan is not run by the common soldier. It is run by the men of money who, behind the scenes, control even the rabid militarists. These gentlemen are not going to see their country devastated, meaning the destruction of their cherished investments. They will seek the opportunity to salvage what they can. So in Germany. So anywhere. The end is in sight. . . .

It seems that Roosevelt will run again. . . . I'm interested to see now who will get the vice presidential nomination. I think it will not be [Henry] Wallace, alas. . . . I think he will be thrown to the wolves as a concession to those who . . . want to express their disapproval of the New Deal and all of its works. I regret this for I think that in the postwar world we need Wallace's international idealism, which is even more apparent than the president's. (How I wish we could sit down after the broadcast and talk and talk about it as we used to do.) . . .

I have had, in common with most of the men out here, a fungus infection, peculiar to the jungle. It settled on my face, and the result is that, by doctor's orders, I have not shaved for some time and have now quite a respectable beard. You would be surprised at the effect. I'm quite distinguished. Beards, and especially mustaches, are not uncommon out here and some are very fancy, indeed. It's hard to tell what war we are fighting. Half of the men look clean-shaven like the Revolutionary army, the rest are either bearded like the Civil War or with handlebar mustaches reminiscent of the Spanish-American. The latter give me a particular pain. . . .

Russell

Monday, July 24, 1944

Dearest family,

You will be interested in a commendation transmitted to me, in a letter to the colonel of our [Engineer] Group, from the 41st Division with which I served in this last operation. It reads as follows:

> While on Temporary Duty with the 163rd Infantry, 41st Inf. Div., Chaplain Stroup at all times conducted himself [so] that his superior devotion to duty is commendable in the highest degree.
>
> The constant efforts of Chaplain Stroup to bring solace and comfort the wounded, and to encourage faith and confidence in the sound, contributed largely to the effectiveness of the soldiers and to the success of their mission. Serving quietly, effectively and without ostentation, he has merited the highest approbation of all personnel. Such superior conduct reflects very favorably on the entire Corps of Chaplains. It is therefore with great pleasure and humble appreciation, that I extend through you to Chaplain Stroup, this commendation of his outstanding services.
>
> By order of Commanding General
41st Infantry Division.

To this Col. Heiman added the following endorsement in sending the communication to me:

> I am happy to note the contents of the basic letter. Your conduct and service with the combat troops will serve as an inspiration to us to do much more each day to give them support.

. . . If my transfer goes through it will be good to return to an outfit that has this feeling about me. . . . We had some good services Sunday, probably my last with the Group. That made it a bit sad and we sang with feeling, "God Be With You Till We Meet Again." While actually I have been with them very little, I have a feeling that they are mine and it is hard to leave them. You know my weakness. . . .

Guess I might as well forget the leave to Australia, and so I'll enclose a money order in this letter because I don't want to carry a lot of bills around with me. . . . Heaven knows, the way I'm jumping around, when your letters will catch up with me, but I'm glad to have heard so recently. All my love.

Russell

While fatigued combat units might be sent on leave to Australia, there was a strict quota on the number of detached officers who could secure leave. Stroup's lobbying for a slot was difficult because it placed him in competition with others.

Another assault task force was being assembled. One unit in this force, the 1st Infantry Regiment of the 6th Division, had done poorly in its first combat exposure. Indeed, the unit's chaplain had been relieved for cowardice. Because of Stroup's combat reputation, the commander decided, just before the regiment's departure, to assign him temporarily to help shape up the unit. The unit would ship to Sansapor on the very western tip of New Guinea, two hundred miles beyond Biak. Stroup's next letter conveys something of his fatigue and disappointment.

Friday, July 28, 1944

Even now the thing has taken on a certain dull monotony. It's hard to recapture the thrill of that first time you sailed into combat. There is the striking of tents and packing of gear. There is the last meal on shore—C-ration or K—hurriedly prepared by harassed mess personnel anxious to get it over with so they can pack their things.

Then the always interminable waiting, like a railway station, only you have no place to sit down and you can't check your packs, and there is no newsstand to engage your attention as you try to select something to while away the hours. The ships in the harbor are going through the endless—and to you meaningless—maneuvers that finally bring them toward the shore in a long line ready to push into the beach and take on their cargo of men. Already there are groups of soldiers waiting in the sand, packs and rifles slung. The Higgins boats will rush in to take men to the converted destroyers that carry the assault troops to shore at that X spot on D day. Back and forward they rush from ship to shore until the beach is empty of men.

Then at some signal flashed from ship to ship, the LCIs [Landing Craft, Infantry] move in, a long line of them traveling at top speed so their momentum will drive them as close as possible to shore. As they move in we move down—long columns of men shuffling slowly along the roads leading to the beach where we take our allotted places at the point where our particular LCI will beach. We watch eagerly their progress, hoping against hope that by some fortunate chance the LCI may get in close enough so that we won't have to wade out waist high or higher in the surf.

Of course they seldom do. Today a wind is blowing the waves in. So we form lines and start out, holding weapons over our heads so they, at least, will be dry. The water hits you. You stumble on the uneven bottom as you stagger toward the gangways that have pushed out from the front of your ship. We climb up the steep slope, our clothes soaked, and water squishing in our shoes. Most of the men have nothing to change into and will stand around until the sun and the wind have dried their clothes. Fortunately I have a change and can get into it, leaving my wet things hung over the rail to dry, which they almost do by night.

By a stroke of bad luck I am in one of the few old-type LCIs in the convoy. That means crowded decks where you squeeze into a corner and try to read, if you have anything to read, or to write as I'm doing now. There are no accommodations for officers. We share the men's quarters below deck—scores of men in every compartment, the bunks in tiers of four deep so closely set together that you can hardly squeeze between them. I sleep in the bottom bunk, four inches from the floor, with just room enough between me and the bunk above to turn over. Each bunk is a piece of canvas lashed to a pipe metal frame—no mattress, no blankets, no pillow. It is too hot to miss blankets. The dozens of men around you lie naked on their bunks—the smell of many men is oppressive in your nostrils. Here you must lie from darkness until dawn for no one is allowed on deck after dark.

Officers and men stand in the chow lines and eat such food as can be prepared from cans with a field stove on an open deck. . . .

The men I am with are from everywhere. Like all soldiers out here they have the slightly pathetic habit of writing the name of their hometown or home state on their caps: Fisherville, Ky.; Detroit; West Bend, Iowa; Bronx, N.Y.; Nebraska; Ohio; etc. . . .

I have something to overcome since the chaplain whose place I am taking was sent back to base because in the little combat this outfit has had, he was afraid. There are not many such, but some. Of course we all are afraid, but some of us don't let it get us down or prevent us from doing our work. The chaplain is the last man who should show fear. . . .

I sent Cranston the Jap flag, finally, and I hope it gets home. It's hard to be certain as things get lost in the mails. There is very little now that you can send home. They have placed an embargo on Japanese guns, for example. I had to turn in the one I rescued for you, as I guess I told you. The flag isn't much, but something. With it is a belt braided by one of the boys out of the cords of the Japanese parachute I had.

Russell

Just two weeks had passed since Stroup left Biak. The next letter is from Sansapor, where the final assault of the New Guinea campaign proved easier than anticipated.

Tuesday, August 1, 1944

Dearest family,

August has come, which means that soon I shall be entering my third year in the army. It seems incredible that only two years have passed since I enlisted—so much has happened. How relative time is and how meaningless our divisions into hours, days, years. Sometimes I doubt whether time has any reality at all. Perhaps God has set Eternity in our hearts to destroy the validity of time. The five years I served in Lynchburg before entering into the service seem so much less than the two years of army life. Pleasant hours pass as moments while the unpleasant plod on weary feet. In Heaven, where we are forever with those who are dear to us, and all joy is ours, even Eternity would seem but a little while.

Still, time marches on and I cannot but regret the years of separation even though I know we will have years together here and hereafter. Not that I count all this time as wasted. There is value in it for me and I try to make the most of it. I refuse to sacrifice years to vain regrets that they were otherwise. Something I will salvage from these days—something of present pleasure and of permanent worth.

You have expressed in several letters the thought that I might be changed by these experiences. I do not think they will alter me for the worse. After all, it is only an intensification of normal life, and one can accept it as such. I am protected by age . . . which gives me a philosophy and a certain fixed character that can be modified but not radically changed.

I'm not sure what it is about this spot in the jungle that induces these vagrant thoughts. It is pleasant enough—much pleasanter in every way than the locale of my last adventure. . . . There is a lovely ocean, a clear and limpid river, and a forest hardly touched by man at all since the Japs had almost no one here. Of course we are busy changing all that, but being with the infantry I am out at the edge of things and some distance from where the engineers are altering the jungle beyond recognition, even after two short days.

The happiest part of it all has been that so far there has been almost no fighting. . . .

I have the strange experience of being deferred to as a veteran by officers and men in this outfit since my experience, limited as it has been, is far greater than theirs. I watch with sophisticated tolerance as they have their first taste of what has almost become commonplace to me. Of course that increases my usefulness as I can speak as one having authority, and that is good for morale. . . .

I had a service on board ship Saturday night before we landed. Sunday being D day there was no opportunity for religious exercises. As always, the service on the eve of uncertainty was an impressive one, and of course my first with any elements of this outfit. . . .

Russell

Monday, August 7, 1944

Dearest family,

I am still here and keeping very busy, although we have had but little action. There are few Protestant chaplains, oddly enough, and I find it difficult to distribute myself around. Yesterday I had four services and each was very well attended. The men were most gratifying in their response. One captain voiced the expressions of many when he said, "It is the best service I have attended since I came into the army, and I can guarantee you that next week there will be three times as many men out." The colonel at one service remarked cynically that the number present was the more remarkable since we had had little action and not much danger. This is a libel on the men, for while it is quite natural that in time of danger they should be present, it does not require that to stimulate interest. A decent interest on the part of the chaplain and something for them when they come is enough to guarantee a good attendance.

The work here had fallen down because the Protestant chaplain who preceded me had made an unenviable reputation for caution and was never found where there might be something popping. There wasn't much opportunity for me to overcome this, since we didn't have much action, but something of my reputation came along with me and I have made it a point to go out with the men on patrols which, while they were not perilous, were the most excitement we had. We did on various patrols run into some Japs, most of whom we took prisoner. This helped to make the men feel that I was with them in their work, and then besides I am considered something of a veteran among these less experienced troops. . . .

You might be interested in the story of one of our patrols. About sixteen men with an officer and myself started out one afternoon on a routine patrol into "enemy country," or at least into country where we had not established ourselves.

We pass out through our lines, making sure that the outposts know we are coming, lest they should see us coming through the jungle and mistake us for Japanese. The men on the perimeter live in pillboxes which they have constructed, digging in well below the surface and roofing their shelters with logs with a slit in front for their weapons. Since there hasn't been much activity we found them sitting around doing their washing, playing cards, talking, or cleaning their weapons. Naturally someone is always on the lookout, but most of them can relax, especially during the day. At night it is different.

Getting beyond them, we wade through a waist-high river, getting good and soaked in the process, and then strike out on a faint trail through the jungle. The going is rather tough with plenty of under-brush and many trailing vines that trip up the unwary. We must go in single file, and every man has his weapon in his hand ready to fire at a moment's notice. The forest is so dense that little light filters through and you progress in a green gloom. The soil underfoot is always damp and there is the constant drip of water from the trees, although the sun is shining. Here and there we skirt a water hole surrounded by mud in which are indented the tracks of crocodiles. Once in a stream we are passing along we see a ten-foot croc go slithering into the water, frightened by our approach. The men are eager to take a shot at him, but that would warn the enemy, if any, that we are around. So the beast is safe.

Every once in a while we come upon a clearing—native gardens— where there are groves of banana and papaua trees. We note certain bunches to pick up on our return trip. There has been little talking along the way, but as we approach a spot where we have reason to believe there might be Japanese all talking ceases and we move with stealth and caution. Finally we halt and send out individuals in a fan ahead to see what they can see. We sit there anxiously waiting for a shot, but none comes.

Eventually, one man returns and whispers that he has discovered a native hut, and two men with a dog, and he thinks they are Japs, although they may be natives. This poses a problem, as we are very careful not to molest the natives and yet we must catch the Japs. The officer orders the men out in a circle to surround the spot, and they disperse, creeping and crawling through the forest. It has started to rain in torrents, which, while it is uncomfortable, works to our advantage since the sound of the rain will cover our approach. The men I am with are on the near side, so we must give the other men time to work around. We go slowly, slipping from tree to tree and bank to bank.

Finally the hut comes in view, very hard to distinguish in the thick forest, made as it is of palm branches. There are two men, clothed, sitting out in front with their backs toward us, apparently eating their meal. A black-and-white dog lies at their feet. It would be easy to shot them where they sit, but we have orders to take prisoners, and besides they just might be natives.

We are close enough now for the dog to catch our scent. He raises up on his hind legs and sniffs inquiringly in our direction. Convinced of danger, he growls, and the men spring up and glance wildly around. They are, without question, Japs. Our officer fires over their heads. His fire is answered by the men around the circle closing in on the hut.

The Nips can plainly tell that they are surrounded. For a moment it seems that they might make a break for it, which would necessitate shooting, but they decide against it and fall on their knees with their hands over their heads.

We continue to close in with caution, for there may be others in the hut. When we are close enough to see that there are not, we come out of concealment and move in on our two prisoners. Naturally they are terrified and are moaning in Japanese, begging for a mercy they do not expect. Their relief when they are not immediately shot is pitiful.

After searching them, we move them back to the rear under guard and hold our position for a while lest other Japs in the vicinity, attracted by the fire, move in. But if they were there, the firing had the opposite effect, and none appear. So we start back with our prisoners.

All of us are wringing wet, our feet slosh in our shoes, and our clothes hang heavy upon us. We do stop, however, to get our bananas. We now have two porters to carry the stalks. Once more we cross the river, which has now become a muddy torrent, taking care to thrash about a good deal to warn off any crocodiles. Now the water is up to our armpits and the poor little Nipponese are nearly drowned before we can haul them over. (The men had suggested that we throw the Nips in first, to see if there were any crocodiles, but this suggestion was not well received by the officer in charge, nor I imagine by the Japanese.) We did have to relieve them of the bananas or they never would have gotten over. I took two bunches on a stick since I had no weapon to carry. As a mater of fact I carried them in the rest of the way, which wasn't far.

We got back about dusk to find that our foxholes were filled with water and our bedding floating around on it, with no dry clothes for a change. That meant bailing out the holes as best we could, wringing out the bedding, and then—with the rain still coming down—lying on the flooded ground in soaking clothes covered by wet bedding to try to sleep. What success the others had I don't know but for myself the night was somewhat restless. . . .

Stroup appreciated that, as the story spread through the task force, it would reinforce the notion that "brave soldiers take prisoners."

I am really quite well and have suffered, so far, none of the aftereffects of D day. . . . I guess that today I am feeling particularly well after a very satisfying Sunday, the results of which compensate for many discomforts. I shall be having services Tuesday, Wednesday, Thursday, and Friday of this week at various organizations, which ought to keep me busy in the evenings. I hadn't really planned for it, but at each group where I spoke yesterday some inquired about having weekday services. Of course I was agreeable to it.

Russell

Good news arrived before the letter was mailed. On the top of the first typewritten page Stroup scribbled, "Looks as though I have my leave to Australia—more later."

Tuesday, August 8, 1944

Dearest family,

Quite out of a clear blue sky and certainly unexpected by me at this time I got orders granting me leave to Sydney, Australia. . . . Of course, having given up hope, I sent the money I had saved home, and now I'll have to secure needed funds, but I'll manage. . . .

When I asked for leave I thought I would be waiting around for orders and might as well be in Australia. Now I'm doing a job where I am needed and rather hate to leave, but of course I can't and wouldn't turn leave down. . . . I'm off—

Russell

The midweek services were deferred until Stroup's return two months later.

Saturday, August 12, 1944

Dearest family,

It's hard for me to believe that I am really here and not simply dreaming. . . . A few days, a few hours ago I was at the front—the farthest outpost—and now I am hundreds of miles from there in a totally different environment and headed for one even more so. . . .

My job was to get to [my assigned] port of embarkation by the given date. The port was more than a thousand miles distant and it was up to me to hitch that distance through jungle, sea, and enemy territory—no small order. Time would not allow me to use a ship all the way, there were no railroads, and a jeep couldn't make it. But luck was with me.

The biggest task was to get out of the combat zone, and I accomplished this by the miracle of getting a ride on a Catalina [flying boat]— a real experience in itself—which carried me the first lap.

. . . These are big boats with plenty of room aboard. . . . It was fascinating to watch the water recede as we gained altitude. The boats in the harbor became smaller and smaller until they crawled below us like toy ships in a baby's bath. I noted that they left paths in the water much as autos do in dirt on the land, stretching far behind them, much further than the wake you can see from the ship itself. . . . We never flew high but kept close to the water, close enough to make out the figure of a man on shore in a canoe. We never got out of sight of land, for part of our job was to patrol the coast as well as carry the mail.

The flight followed the north coast of New Guinea eastward to Maffin Bay, from which Stroup had departed two weeks earlier.

From the air you can see far down into the water, and as you fly along you note the coral reefs submerged but visible. The varying depths give different colors to the sea, and there was a beautiful patchwork of every shade of blue and green—a lovely sight. Where rivers joined the sea you could mark how the fresh water flowed far out to sea. There were many rivers. High up on the mountains which fringed the coastline, waterfalls tumbled out of the clouds into green depths of forest. We had the sky to ourselves all the way.

I took a place back in the tail where, through the gun "blisters" on each side, you could gain the best view. . . . We drifted into a number of bays where Japs might be found, but, to the disappointment of the gunners, none appeared. They did limber up the guns a bit, firing at schools of sharks. We all took a try at it. The plane flew very steadily so it wasn't difficult to hold your stance at the gun, but the weapon itself jumped a good deal when you let off a salvo of bullets, so it wasn't easy to hit the target. Whether or not I got any sharks I don't know as we didn't stop to check. . . .

Close to sunset we came toward our destination, so well known to me but strange now as seen from the air. . . . I had arrived at my old stamping grounds. . . .

The next morning luck was still with me and I caught a C-47 that carried me a long ways south in another five hours' flying. I spent the night at a great air center and took off the next morning, landing at a port some distance from my destination, where I hoped to catch a ship that was sailing there. I now had time enough to go by water the rest of the way. . . .

Stroup had probably been ordered to report to a ship at Port Moresby on the south coast of New Guinea near its western tip, as far from Sansapor as it was possible to travel around the coast of that island. He had reached Finschhafen, a port far to the east.

I learned that there was no ship sailing to my assigned port of departure. However there was a ship, sailing in two hours, taking men on leave directly to Australia. There was room for me on board since one officer had failed to show up. This meant . . . I could sail without charge to my destination, arriving there a week before I would have otherwise. . . .

By night I was comfortably ensconced on a lovely little Norwegian ship, eating a delicious meal with fresh meat and ice cream, with the prospect of restful days at sea ahead of me and fifteen days of leave at the end of the way. . . .

Russell

Sunday, August 13, 1944

Dearest family,

Today being Sunday and there being two chaplains on board we planned to have two services. But the ocean, forgetting that the Sabbath should be a day of calm, acted up. The other chaplain took to his bunk. He gave forth, but his outpourings were from the physical man, so I had to assume the burden of the spiritual alone. Our congregations were invisible since no one wanted to be on deck. I had to conduct the service over the public address system. . . .

All the officers on the ship, passengers that is, were given certain jobs to do—inspecting mess, censoring letters, managing companies, etc. We two chaplains were included. I was happy to do what I could, my job being to manage the mess line. But shortly after sailing the colonel in command came to me and said I was relieved from duty. When I inquired why, he said that the other chaplain had reminded him that no chaplain could be given "secular duties." If he were given such duties he would have to make mention of it in his monthly report, which eventually would mean trouble for the colonel. I begged him to allow me to continue, which he agreed to do provided I understood it was voluntary. I had no intention of sitting about idle while some other officer shouldered an extra share of the duties.

You see how some of our chaplains endear themselves to the command. This particular brother came to me with the tale of how he had set the colonel wise. He hoped for my commendation and thanks. I told him what I thought, but he still failed to turn a hand to help. Today, of course, due to sickness, he couldn't assume even sacred duties. . . .

I don't suppose I shall ever lose my zest for ocean travel. Always it relaxes me, body and spirit, as few other things will do. . . . It would be really quite perfect if only you all could be at the other end. . . . Hasten the day. . . .

Russell

Before the war, Stroup took vacations from his duties as parish minister and the confinement of living with his mother and brother. From Lynchburg, when he could seize a few days, he would take a train to New York City for a binge of plays, concerts, and art galleries. Because money was tight, he would buy standing-room tickets, and at night he would often sleep on the subway rather than renting a room. My impression is that as a young man he was shy and remained a loner on these excursions, though after the war he would meet his wife-to-be on such a New York City outing.

A serviceman's vacation in Sydney, Australia, was quite a different experience, as Stroup describes—with bitter humor—in the following letter. The only "binge" available was of a character he would not choose, leaving him at loose ends. Perhaps he did not fully appreciate how depressed he was from combat and, indeed, how depressed other servicemen may have been as well. There was neither time nor facilities for real therapy, and to lose oneself in a brief "binge" was helpful for many. Stroup did not find the culture he had enjoyed on other vacations, and he apparently remained too shy to reach out for suitable contacts that might have nurtured him.

A week following the previous letter, Stroup wrote on American Red Cross stationery. He was housed in the Red Cross Club, sharing a room with three other officers.

Tuesday, August 22, 1944

Dearest family,

There was a lively discussion by the officers on the boat coming down on the subject, "What does a chaplain do on his leave?" The consensus of opinion was that unless he could forget he was a chaplain or disguise the fact, his two weeks would be very dreary ones. Of course they felt that leave for them held everything desirable, but when I pressed them for elaboration it seemed that their pleasure would consist of eating, drinking, and women—a dreary outlook, but not in their eyes.

Well apparently the government, and particularly the Red Cross, holds the same point of view. Everything is done to make it possible for you to get "eats," liquor, and gals. . . . There is no provision made for anyone who digresses from the norm. . . .

I have enjoyed eating my fill of fresh meat, eggs, baked goods, pastry, ice cream, etc. By now, however, I could do with a bit of variety. This place is so 100 percent Anglo-Saxon that there are not even Greek restaurants . . . to say nothing of French, Spanish, Chinese. . . . The Red Cross Clubs profess to have the best food in the city, and I guess they do, but here enters the second difficulty. They have it firmly in mind that soldiers are yearning for steaks, hamburgers, plain milk, malted milk, pie à la mode, and Coca-Cola. The result is that EVERY night there is steak and French fried potatoes. I will not yearn for a steak for a long time to come. At each place setting they smirkingly set a bottle of milk, and they become first incredulous and then offended when I ask them to please take it away. Every desert is pie à la mode or banana splits, and for lunch there is hamburger.

Even the natives have been indoctrinated. When they ask me if I want a "sweet" and I say I do they archly suggest pie à la mode and are astonished that I should refuse it. One waitress insisted on bringing it anyhow, thinking I must have been fooling. . . .

The liquor I must pass up, but it is difficult as you are given a certain weekly ration of the stuff, and if you don't draw it commotion results— the theory being, no doubt, that if you haven't called for your supply you must have been foully murdered in some dark alley. Actually, the amount of hard liquor allowed is very small, although beer and wine are adequate. . . .

As for the ladies, I would not object to some sort of feminine companionship if it were available, but certainly not the sort that is obtained through the Red Cross or any other means at my disposal. The girls are very pretty, many of them, but the ones on Red Cross "dating" lists are hardly the ones I might be interested in and there is no time for me to get in touch with others. Oddly enough, I have felt only a mild interest and have not missed this, to most, PRIMARY essential of a successful leave. In fact no effort whatever is made by the Red Cross, which controls everything, to provide for the needs of a civilized individual who might be interested in good conversation with agreeable companions who have brains. . . .

This great metropolis of a pioneer country—about where America was one hundred years ago—has almost nothing cultural to offer. The principal entertainments are movies and dances. One lone stock company puts on plays—I've seen the current one and enjoyed it very much—but beyond that nothing. Once in a while there is music. I have heard of no lectures. The art galleries are pitiful and the libraries rare. I have enjoyed the bookstores and have bought and read quite a number of books. This has been wonderful, as I was literally starved in my mind. . . .

Everyone is so very thoughtful it is difficult to enjoy yourself. I have longed for a chance to be alone. But even in the restaurants, let me get comfortably seated at a table with a good meal and a good book and some considerate soul, taking pity on my aloneness, brings over another officer. I tried to find a hotel in a nearby community but without success until today, when I was able to book a room in a place some fifty miles away where I hope and pray there will be no Red Cross and no servicemen so I can rest and refresh my soul.

This may sound as though I weren't enjoying myself, which isn't true. . . . I could expatiate on the glories of a barbershop where I had "the works," or a Turkish bath that almost got rid of the accumulated dirt of the months, or the horse race I saw Saturday, or the lovely church services I attended Sunday. There was a surprising number of American soldiers, sailors, aviators, and nurses at the church service and I was proud of them. I have also met our men in the bookstores of the city and at the art galleries, etc.

Russell

Hotel Camberra, Saturday, August 26, 1944

Dearest family,

This seems to be what I was seeking. Here are peace and quiet: almost no army, and freedom to do as I please in comfort. The only hardship is a lack of central heating in the hotel: I am reminded of England where you crawl into incredibly cold sheets at night and never truly warm up until morning. The only solutions are matrimony or a bed warmer.

Here are rolling fields surrounded by hills. There are cows and horses and sheep in the meadows—always sheep. I enjoy watching the sheepdogs work. Since I arrived yesterday I have spent most of my time walking paths across country and stopping to rest in the sun, to revel in the views, to dream, or maybe to read a book. I watch the clouds go by and think of home. It's a bucolic existence and just what I've wanted. Unfortunately the hotel could give me a room for four days only.

I report for my return trip on September second, and then wait for transportation—days or even weeks. I'm in no hurry to get back, so long as I arrive in time for the next push. We will be going forward in the not-too-distant future. All that seems remote from here, yet I know that this is only an interlude. I feel guilty to have it, but I think I'll be able to do a better job because of it.

Russell

[from Sydney, several days later]

. . . [in Camberra] I went to St. Andrew's Church on Sunday morning. There the minister asked me to take the evening service. I enjoyed that very much. It is a lovely church with a nice congregation. They were most appreciative of my effort and asked me to return, which of course I cannot. After the service, in typical English fashion we had "supper," a nice, jovial time. Everyone was cordial, and most appreciative of what America has done for Australia. . . .

Russell

Tuesday, September 5, 1944

Dearest family,

. . . As Doctor Meltzer had suggested when I left [Sansapor], today I had a thorough physical checkup, because the facilities here are more complete. So far as I know the results are satisfactory, and I'll get the complete report tomorrow. After so many months in the tropics this was a good idea, although I hate to have doctors messing over me.

Last Sunday evening the pastor of a Presbyterian church in the suburbs asked me to preach for him. I consented with some reluctance since this was the "King's Day of Prayer." However we had a nice congregation and they were most appreciative. I did well and they recognized the fact. Several were good Scottish people with thick brogues, pleasant to hear. I was glad for another chance to preach to an Australian congregation. It feels good to be in the pulpit again.

The war news continues to be wonderful. (Reading the papers here, of course, one would imagine that the British were winning the battle for France with some help from a few Americans.) What comes after the war worries me more. I do not see that we have evolved a real plan. There is no expression of, as Abraham Lincoln put it, "with malice toward none, with charity toward all, with firmness in the right as God gives us to see the right, let us finish the task." Most people say: let's be so hard on Germany and Japan that they will learn their lesson and never cause trouble again. This psychology is wrong. All an enemy learns from that approach is that it is a very bad thing to lose a war.

If, by our treatment of them, we could help them feel that more is to be gained by peace than by war, we might accomplish something. There is only one way to destroy an enemy and that is to make him a friend. The men here, however, don't see that.

I think that when peace has been won in Europe I will immediately apply for a discharge. Not only my desire but my duty calls me back. I can do more there than here when the boys start coming home and people begin working on plans for peace in a new world. That, however, will be several months away. In the meantime I will continue to serve here, probably actively.

This month includes both Margretta's and Richard's birthdays, and I shall be thinking of them so much. At home it is also fall, my favorite season, though it is spring out here. For me the glory of autumn will be reserved for next year. It is wonderful to feel that by then, certainly, there will be peace.

Russell

Monday, September 11, 1944

Dearest family,

The return voyage is on the same ship that brought me down and with substantially the same group of men. Yesterday we had a service on board with three chaplains taking part, including one Negro chaplain who is making the trip with us.

I think I established an American record while on leave, since in all the time I was in Australia I didn't have a date or a drink. I wouldn't have objected to the former but cared so little that I made no effort, and remained quite happy. The Australian girls are attractive and something more than willing, but somehow it was hard for me to think that way.

I think that there are two possible reactions on leave from combat. One is to get far away from it all in a wild time with wine, women, and song. The other—mine—precludes any of these. I just couldn't bring myself to indulge. The memories were too fresh for that.

Stroup sought solitude for healing, yet I wish he might have allowed a human touch as well.

However, I did enjoy myself seeing new country, sleeping in real beds, eating real food at tables with linen, china, and silver, reading a lot of books, visiting art galleries, parks, zoos, etc. I did what I wanted without thought for anyone else. Above all I was alone, away from dirt and noise and misery. It was *good.* I am now ready to go back to whatever lies ahead.

By the way, the results of my physical checkup were very satisfactory. They could find nothing wrong.

Russell

Thursday, September 14, 1944

Dearest family,

Today we have been sailing through the familiar waters of the New Guinea seas. They are lovely. As the ship moves cautiously across submerged coral reefs, the water is transformed from deep blue to opalescent greens.

Now it is velvet night scattered with diamond stars and, fittingly enough, we have come to anchor in a harbor ringed with shore lights whose reflections, along with the running lights of ships, dance on the water. Our ship's engine has ceased to throb. The quiet comes as a benediction to the day. On deck you can smell the familiar stench of the jungle. Somehow it loses its unpleasantness when it brings back memories of eventful days.

Russell

Friday, September 22, 1944

Dearest family,

I am still on my way. The leave ship dropped me off at a southern New Guinea port. We were warned that it might be days, even weeks, before transportation was available north but my luck was extraordinary, as usual. After only one night and a Sunday morning, I found passage on a ship headed north to the port [Biak] where for so many weeks I suffered, bled, and died with the 41st Division. This suited me fine, for I wanted to stop there to discover my transfer status. If the request had gone through, I could just remain.

The trip was most pleasant on a new Liberty ship that was well appointed. My greatest joy was a well-stocked library. The vessel had been named for a certain gentleman whose daughter launched the ship and, in appreciation, donated a fine collection of modern books. Most of them were a bit beyond the interest of merchant seamen, but some were just my meat. I read several on the short four days of our voyage—a feast to be preferred even to the lobster we were served.

My reception from the headquarters chaplain's staff has been enthusiastic, and even more so from the officers of the 3d Battalion with whom I labored so long. I was disappointed to learn, however, that my request for transfer to the 41st, which they had endorsed, has not been approved. I remain on duty with the 6th Division. Yet the 6th is a good division and I like the men there. Perhaps I would feel as fondly toward them as I do toward the 3d Battalion, 163d Infantry, 41st Division, if we had been through as much together. A bond is established in combat that I feel most keenly.

Things have changed a lot since I left [Biak]. It is a settled post with good roads, encampments with wooden floors in the tents, and other refinements. You don't have to spend time in foxholes. There are movies and libraries.

I was sitting in the chaplain's office when a call came to go to the cemetery for a burial, and as I was the only chaplain present I went, remembering the many times I had gone to that sad place, and recalling the pathetic little crosses in an unkempt cemetery surrounded by artillery, the peace of which was shattered by our own guns and by raids from the Japanese. I remembered trying to bring some ceremony and dignity to the services with a little group of ragged, battle-stained men around an open grave into which we lowered the blanket-wrapped body of a comrade. After the service I would stand at attention and, by hand salute, pay the honors required to one who had "borne the brunt of the battle" [Abraham Lincoln].

I arrived there today to find a neatly fenced cemetery that would be lovely anywhere. A flag flew at half-mast from the pole, and there was a chapel where the funeral party was gathered. The dead lad was in a fine casket draped with the flag. We had service in the chapel and at the grave with all religious and military pageantry. A squad of rifles gave the salute and a bugler blew taps. No raiding Jap planes disturbed the internment.

To me, however, the service was not as meaningful as before. Afterwards I moved among the crosses where I had laid so many lads to rest, and I found myself deeply stirred by the memories of days that in my mind were just yesterday, but by appearances must have occurred years ago.

The colonel of the 3rd Battalion asked me if I had received my decoration and when I asked "What decoration?" told me that he had recommended the Silver Star for gallantry in action regarding the [road to Damascus] incident. I appreciate his recommendation, however little it may be deserved. Compared to what others did here I have no right to it, I know, although I presume medals have been given for less.

Russell

Because the following letter contained profanity, Stroup addressed it to his brother alone. This was a signal to his mother that, by choosing to read it, as of course she would, she waived her right to be offended.

Sunday, September 24, 1944

Dear Cranston,

On this Sabbath I have just completed a most satisfactory morning. Several days ago the division chaplain asked me to take the service. As it turned out, we have fine USO entertainers here: a quartet of two men and two women, accompanied by a lady on the piano, singing classical and semiclassical music. The soldiers have responded well, in part because the young ladies, who might not be considered great beauties back home, here appear to be a combination of Cleopatra, Delilah, and Ginger Rogers.

After one entertainment I asked if they would sing at my service on Sunday. They agreed: one young woman sang Ave Maria and the other the Lord's Prayer, while the tenor led congregational singing. They were good, and of course they filled the chapel. The division chaplain realized his mistake too late, and the best he could do was to claim a part in the program, while allowing me to preach as he had requested.

I preached a pretty good sermon—the first one the general and chief of staff, as well as many others, had heard for a long time.

There has been resentment among the officers that the senior staff has been monopolizing the young ladies. The younger officers feel this is unfair not only to them but to the young ladies themselves. A few planned a most successful revenge. They recruited one of the little native boys, an engaging "fuzzy-wuzzy" without benefit of English, and coached him in his role. The traveling artists had finished dinner with the general and his staff and, when they emerged from the tent, there had gathered a crowd of men waiting to see, not the general, but the young ladies. In front of the crowd was a grinning little native lad holding a bunch of wildflowers, obviously for the ladies. The general, vastly pleased, escorted the fairest of the three toward this tableaux. Beckoning the little fellow forward, he urged him in English that the boy could not understand to present the floral tribute to the young lady. Quite at ease, the lad moved forward, lifted up the flowers, and with a charming grin delivered in singsong English the words of greeting he had learned from the obliging officers. In the silence, "General is goddamn sonofabitch" fell on astonished ears.

Let us draw the curtain on this touching scene.

Russell

6

"I Would Like to Write Something Really Constructive"

The next letter, written three days later, was mailed from Sansapor. On the envelope Stroup wrote a new army address. All envelopes since his arrival in the South Pacific had given "1112 Engr. Combat Group" as the return address. Now he wrote from the 1st Battalion Headquarters, 1st Infantry Regiment, 6th Infantry Division. The letter inside detailed the complex army politics that led to this transfer.

Wednesday, September 27, 1944

Dearest family,

I want to get my permanent address to you at once. Please give it to the church people as well. If I'm lucky this will remain for some time, this or something like it—I'm not sure whether I'll remain at the 1st Battalion. At the moment I'm detailed to regimental headquarters since the regimental chaplain, a Catholic, has gone on leave to Australia. I have the regiment to myself for a while.

Let me explain why I am here. You will remember that just before I was assigned temporary duty with the 6th Division in order to make the landing here, I had put through a request for permanent transfer from the 111 2th Engineers to the 41st Division with which I served [on Biak]. The 111 2th was slow to forward this request up the chain of command. Meanwhile, my work with the 1st Infantry Regiment here [on Sansapor] had made such an impression on the commanding officer that he sent up a request that I be assigned to them permanently. This request was approved by the 6th Division and sent up to the 6th Army. My earlier request to transfer to the 41st Division also reached the 6th Army, but it arrived too late. Technically I have been a member of the 1st Infantry Regiment since August 18, but I knew nothing of all this until I returned from Australia.

I assume that the result is for the best. Truly, I do like this organization and know I shall be happy here. While I was away, the colonel in command of the 1st Regiment took sick and was replaced temporarily by my friend Lt. Col. Corbin. A new full colonel has just arrived but Corbin remains second in command. This gives me what I did not have before—a friend in the regimental headquarters. Indeed, today the division chaplain told me that Corbin is insistent that I be made regimental chaplain even though I am outranked in point of service by other chaplains. Whether he will have his way I do not know. I do know that Corbin arranged my transfer directly to the 1st Regiment, rather than to the 6th Division where the division chaplain would have authority to assign me to whatever regiment he thought best. This was an unusual procedure, but the colonel was taking no chances.

In addition, my friend Major Vance has been taken from the 1st Battalion and made commanding officer of the 2d Battalion, so I now have a good friend in charge there as well. Major Vance wants me with his battalion, but Col. Corbin wants me at headquarters. For the time being I am at headquarters. I have a nice tent down by the seaside with all comforts and conveniences. All the officers and men have been most cordial: you would think that I had been with them for years. During my previous short stay with them I seem to have made a lot of friends.

My military career has certainly provided a variety of experiences. The 100th Division [with which Stroup trained in South Carolina] was a new division without any background. [On Biak] the 41st was a National Guard outfit with traditions rooted in the states from which the men came. The 6th, here, is an old army division. Within it the 1st Infantry Regiment, as the name implies, was the first infantry unit in the U.S. Army, dating back to the Revolution. Its rich store of traditions is unequaled. There are some old-timers who remember service in the Philippines, China, etc. There is an elaborate coat of arms, and battle flags with many battle ribbons. Most of the officers, and the chaplains, are regular army, and there is a decided esprit de corps. So far in this war they have not done much fighting: enough so the men are not green, but nothing to match the 41st Infantry.

Before I left [Biak] I learned from the major and the lieutenant colonel why I had not received my medal. The regimental chaplain—

a lad who never did like me and who had served a long time without recognition, because he was always way back to the rear—had stopped my citation and never forwarded it to the general. The major and the colonel said they would initiate the process again. Tell Cranston he doesn't have to use harsh words about the regimental chaplain since the major and colonel used them all and with more fluency than Cranston can muster. It remains incongruous that the men who were with me on the Jericho road should all have received Bronze Stars and I, who was their leader, received nothing.

All such military politics were overshadowed by news that the most important article Stroup had written from the South Pacific had been accepted for publication—thanks, apparently, to editing by his sister and literary contacts made by his brother.

I found just scores of letters here when I arrived, from the last of June to the seventh of September. I am thrilled that *Harper's* has accepted my article, and I hope for more such news. How in the world does Margretta find time to edit my stuff? I think that my essay on the hardships of military life is one of the best and ought to find a home somewhere, but aside from Cranston's good comments I have received no encouragement.

Russell

The essay on hardships has been lost, but Stroup's article in the October issue of Harper's, *entitled "A Soldier Looks at the Church," would cause something of a sensation. It was most likely written shortly after Stroup's experience of intense combat on Biak, for he wrote from a fresh perspective. Stroup had always been a son of the Church, grounded in his mother's piety, in his father's remarkably successful ministry, and in his own Jesus-centered spirituality. Nevertheless, in this essay he wrote, first of all, as a soldier.*

He began: "To the question, 'What does the soldier think of the Church?' the only proper answer is 'He doesn't.'" The problem was not that the soldier lacked religious feeling or interest. "Religion . . . is one of his favorite topics of conversation. To his long and lively discussions he brings an eager interest and an incredible ignorance. His faith is far greater than his knowledge."

The problem was how the churches presented themselves, a problem compounded by the poor preparation of their chaplains. "It is distressing,"

The Great Powers and Europe

October

Harper's
MAGAZINE

HARPER & BROTHERS, PUBLISHERS

Secret Mission to Rome

Stroup wrote, "to see the perturbation of many Army chaplains thrown for the first time into intimate contact with the rank and file of Americans for whom the Church simply does not exist." Soldiers expected chaplains to be censorious of their venal sins—drinking, cursing, whoring, and the like—but did not expect help from chaplains with their deepest concerns. Combat soldiers know that

> *the awful necessity of war has made them wreckers and killers. They have been taught to shoot, stab, and throttle their enemies. They have been exiled from peaceful homes and the creative work they knew to live like rats in muddy holes. They feel instinctively that the physical and spiritual suffering of war in which they have shared must result from the sins of the world. They would like to know what these sins are. They would like to hear them condemned in themselves as well as others. They long to understand the reason for the cross on which they hang and that other Cross where goodness, justice, mercy, beauty, honor, and love are crucified. They desperately hope that the world may be saved; but how? And the Padre says, "Naughty, naughty for getting drunk."*

Stroup continued with an elaboration of some ideas expounded in his letters. "The voice of the Church should have been raised against the evils that breed wars." On the other hand, he reiterated, we must affirm, not condemn, the motives of those who must fight. "They are laying the gift of themselves upon the altar as a sacrifice to what they believe to be ideals worth dying for. . . . There is one good thing which war, the destroyer, creates, and that is the righteous purpose in the hearts of men to give themselves freely for what they conceive to be some higher good."

To prepare for peace, churches must purge themselves of racism, sexism, authoritarianism, and materialism, Stroup continued. "Until the Church has put into practice the basically Christian standard of 'from every man according to his ability and to every man according to his need' we shall not be able to lead the world in a Christian solution of our economic problems." (The Christian-Socialist influence of his childhood home is revealed in his unself-conscious paraphrase of Karl Marx to summarize Christian ethics.)

Most important, churches must cease trying to control what people think. "The hope of humanity lies in the untrammeled search for Truth. This alone can set men free. In this search the Church should lead the way. . . . Only as we allow the winds of freedom to blow unchecked in our own communions will men recognize our leadership in a democratic world."

Another genre of Stroup's writing—his letters to the families of those he had buried—would bear healing fruit.

Dearest family,

It was you, Mother, who reminded me how much the messages I send to bereaved families might comfort them. I am beginning to receive replies, and you may be interested. One mother writes, "Dearest Chaplain, There are not enough words in the world to tell you how happy I am to hear from you regarding my son Milton. To tell God's truth I was in bed ever since the news came, but when I heard from you I got right out of bed and walked again. . . . What you and those comrades of his have done for him will never be forgotten by me. Please tell every one that knew my son how grateful I am, and that they helped a distracted mother back to health again."

Another writes, "Words can never express my gratitude to you for writing. I am so thankful that my son had a Christian burial. Even the smallest details mean all the world to me. . . . May God bless you and reward you according to His riches in Glory. . . . I'd love to see that grave by the sea where my boy is sleeping now. . . . My husband passed away in July 1943 and I have only one other son, a twin of Bernie's, also in the service. My heart is bleeding and broken but I know God doeth all things well."

The wife of an aviator writes, "It means so much to know that my husband's body was found and properly laid to rest. Since the War Department notified me of his death I've been tortured by visions of his body lying neglected under the tropic sun. . . . Will you please tell me all about his resting place? . . . Thank you, thank you for your kind letter. . . . It is hard for me to realize that he will not return, but I must accept the truth of his death and continue to live for our baby who he never saw."

And so they go. These are some of the satisfactions of this service. One such letter pays for all the pain of those days. . . .

I've always known that it paid to have a good literary agent and I could hardly have found a better one to take care of my interests than Cranston. He surely did a swell job [with *Harper's*] and I agree that half of the honorarium should be his by rights. We can both enjoy it when I get home.

With regard to publishing my letters, I think that they would have to be cleared with the War Department, but I really don't know about the regulations. The best thing to do would be to submit them to the chief of chaplain's office before publication, if a magazine insists. . . .

The Sansapor beach and the surrounding airfields were now one of the huge staging areas where troops were assembling for the invasion of the Philippines—a logistical operation second only to preparations for the Normandy landing in Europe.

I'm glad that you know where I am. You guessed my last two stopping places, including this one, without a word from me. This place has tremendous trees, but the undergrowth is not dense. The trees provides plenty of shade and lots of lumber. My tent is shaded at the edge of the forest, with only the beach between me and the ocean. There's a strong cool breeze blowing off the sea, although it is mighty hot in the sun—we are almost on the Equator.

As I look out I can see a native outrigger canoe going by with a large Dutch flag flying as a precaution against being fired upon. There is little fighting going on, although every day they bring in some Japanese prisoners, and some are killed. We have had very few deaths from enemy fire since we landed here.

When our new colonel outlined his policies to the officers yesterday, he gave the chaplains quite a buildup. Privately he told me that he intended to do everything he could to help us in our work. He is a West Point graduate, strictly GI, demanding lots of spit and polish—much more than is usual this far forward, so some of us will have to remember to salute again. He gets us up early in the morning and keeps us going all day. This suits me fine since my "going" can be at the typewriter where I look busy but am writing to you.

You refer a number of times to my coming home. I don't know how it can be arranged. My friend Dr. Meltzer, age forty-five, just got turned down under the thirty-eight-years-and-over clause. When the war ends in Europe, that should make a difference. What I plan is to wait until I am forty, the war in Europe is over, and we have gotten into the Philippines. That should all come about the same time— the psychological time to strike. I will have been overseas for more than a year, which will help, and I will have one more campaign to my credit. It may be that I can make it by next spring, certainly by October. . . .

We have been expecting General Krueger from the 6th Army to drop in on us all day, and I just learned that he is in the area. I'd better get this letter out of the typewriter or he might ask to see what I have been writing, which would be embarrassing.

Russell

P.S. Glad you got the Jap flag.

Monday, October 2, 1944

Dearest family,

Yesterday was a good one for me. I had two services, each followed by a communion service—it being the first Sunday of the month. All were well attended. An especially large number remained for communion, partly because so many of the men are Lutherans. The bulk of this regiment came originally from Missouri, Iowa, the Dakotas, Minnesota, etc.—good stock. This includes a lot of men of German and Scandinavian descent, which means Lutherans. We are still holding most of our services in the open air.

Russell

Friday, October 5, 1944

This letter begins with a concerned response to news that Cranston had traveled to Johns Hopkins University Hospital for tests related to his encephalitis. Apparently I, at the age of ten, accompanied him on the train to Washington. The trip was beset by delays before we were met there by my mother.

Cranston and Richard, having similar natures, must have been fit to be tied by the time they got off the train at Washington. (Cranston won't like that comparison. I mean, of course, that they are both nervous under strain.) . . .

A Methodist chaplain from one of the Air Corps groups called on me yesterday because he had seen my article, "Fear in the Shadows," from the *Presbyterian Outlook*. The editor, Aubrey Brown, wrote me that he had supplied several thousand reprints to Methodist, Episcopal, and Presbyterian denominations to be distributed to their chaplains, and this nice person had just received his.

The article was a scathing denunciation of those who preach "hellfire" to combat soldiers. It began,

In the valley of the shadow of death there are chaplains, God forgive them, preaching the "gospel" of fear. Fortunately, they are few; but some there are, as in the churches back home, who raise the grim specter of death and fan the fires of hell, hoping to compel the men to seek the Father who has assured us that in that dark valley we need not be afraid. Some shivering little souls may be won that way, but real men—and most men out here in the South Pacific are that—instinctively turn with disgust from such a perversion of the saving gospel of Jesus Christ whose perfect love casts out all fear.

Fear is an evil thing. You do not inspire that which is high and holy by appealing to that which is low and base. Soldiers know that, for they have been afraid. Facing agony and death, they have met the coward that lies hidden in the heart of every man and have hated him. Their one noble fear is that they may be afraid. How, then, can they have patience with preaching that is based on an emotion they loathe for its shameful power to degrade a man?

Nor are they moved by threats. It is not a question of whether or not they believe in hell. They have lived, many of them, in its borderland. But a threat is no less odious because it is backed by reality. Tell a real man that unless he accepts Christ he will go to hell, and he may believe you, but will nonetheless stubbornly reject salvation on terms that would compromise his manhood. I have known many more men who rejected Christ because they faced death than I have men who accepted him for that reason. Rightly or wrongly, they refused to be moved by the threat of danger to do what they had not done before. Again and again soldiers have said to me, "After I get out of this, I'll be a Christian; but not now." . . .

I heard a lot of tommyrot talked in the States about men accepting God in foxholes because they were afraid. Someone who knows these men should kill that damnable lie. I have seen many men give themselves to Christ in the combat zone, but they were not driven by fear or compelled by threats. They were sobered by reality, chastened by adversity, challenged by Divinity. Had an attempt been made to frighten or threaten, they would have turned away.

The true appeal of Christ is not to men's craven fears but to their highest courage. He does not speak to the coward that crouches in every man's heart, but to the hero that lives in every man's soul. . . . When we say to men, "God needs you and his Kingdom tarries on your coming," they will leave all and follow him. When we approach them not with threats but a challenge we will be talking their language. When we offer them not security but sacrifice—a sacrifice of themselves for humanity—then they will deny themselves and take up a cross. . . .

They are eager for a faith to live by, but it must be a faith for life and not for death. They know how to die! We must show them how to live. The meanest of them can die nobly. To live nobly is another matter, and they know that. Having faced death they appreciate how precious life can be and they want passionately to live it to the full, if it is granted to them. . . .

We must cause them to fall in love with Christ. They cannot be herded to him by the lash of fear. But they can be won to him by the power of Love. How susceptible men are to that power in its earthly form is abundantly apparent in every lonely bivouac and battlefield where men find that all that makes life sweet is contained in memories of wives and sweethearts, home and children, parents and friends. If, in spite of all that war can do to them, these men keep pure, tender, strong, brave, noble and loving it is because of the sweet compulsion of the affection of those who hold their hearts in thrall. It is the one appeal that cannot fail; for love never faileth. Hearts impervious to fear are touched to tenderness by love.

Why are we blind to the uses of that power? We argue with men about the truth of God, and their minds are closed against us. We threaten men with the wrath of God, and their wills stubbornly resist. But it is the Love Unknown that breaketh every barrier down; for God came in Christ not to change men's minds or to break their wills, but to touch their hearts. He is in Christ, loving the world unto himself. . . .

In December 1944 this article was also reprinted in an ecumenical journal, The Chaplain, *that was distributed to all Protestant chaplains in the military. Stroup's letter of October 5 concluded with this apt story:*

I dropped into a mess hall in the 3d Battalion today and asked for a meal. The mess sergeant said, "After that service you gave us Sunday you can have anything you want!"

Russell

Friday, October 12, 1944

Dearest family,

Tonight is prayer meeting night and I've just returned from the service. We had almost a hundred men there and it was held in just one of the battalions. Chaplain Steinenger had a service in the other, and the third is reached on Wednesday. It isn't nice to mention it, but the chaplain had eight men at his service. This is pitiful, and alas too common throughout the army. He's a nice fellow but, like too many chaplains and preachers, bone lazy as far as his work is concerned. He stays as far away from the men as possible, never shares in their work, and is dismayed that our new colonel expects us to be out with the field exercises.

Another type of chaplain I've met here increasingly is the disgusting type who has departed from his roots: drinking, gambling, being "a regular guy." Most of these are timid souls who didn't dare say "Boo" at home; they have so little self-respect that they can't handle freedom when it's offered to them. They were good before because they had to be.

I didn't mean to get off on the weaknesses of my brethren. I'm not one to judge since I am never tempted to do those things and so have no reason to be other than I am. My temptations, and my sins, are more subtle. Nevertheless, I can't help hating stupidity and weakness. I should be more charitable.

I meant to describe the setting for our service tonight. We have built a theater in the open, just benches under the sky on a high bluff overlooking the sea. There we gathered. You can look out over the gray-green ocean to a promontory of wooded hills across the waters. There was violet in the evening haze, then behind it flamed a glorious sunset of rose and gold and gray. Truly the glory of the Lord shone round about us. The sunset faded as the service proceeded, and when we had finished it was quite dark with stars shining above the tall trees shading us, and with the ocean below us. A service in such a setting was bound to be impressive.

Today I said good-bye to the 1112th Engineers [who were, apparently, departing from Sansapor]. Yesterday I had a service with them, which was quite moving because we all felt that it might be a long time, or perhaps forever, before we were together again. Meanwhile, who knows what we might go through. They are a fine bunch of men and I shall not forget them. This time our situations are reversed: they precede and I follow. Heretofore I have always been ahead of them. I feel cheated.

The last few days I have been working on an assignment by the colonel. He put a lot of material in my hands and told me to write up a history of the regiment for the benefit of the replacements we are getting in. I found it most interesting to read the record of the 1st Regiment, organized in 1784 at the same time as our country, and in action ever since.

Under the motto "Semper Primus" (Always First), Stroup's ten-page, mimeographed, morale-building history began:

> This is the story of a Regiment, but it is more than that. It is the story of a Nation, for the history of the First Infantry is the history of America. The First Infantry shared in the nation's creation, made possible her expansion, fought for her preservation and contributed to her greatness.

Stroup concluded this letter of October 12 with a suggestion for his own comfort.

I'm going to make a peculiar request. Please send me two single sheets and two suits of pajamas, without buttons. With jeep and trailer, I have a place to carry them. While no one else uses such, I get irritated by wool blankets next to my skin.

Russell

Wednesday, October 17, 1944

Dearest family,

So many have commented on the fact that the attendance at Sunday services has increased amazingly of late. I can't speak for what it was before, but it really has been most unusual and I am deeply gratified by it. I had two services Sunday, in the morning and in the evening. Today I go to a rather distant outpost by water and meet with a company, and Thursday will be our midweek service.

Now is the time, in these weeks of training, for me to get to know the men and help to prepare them for the spiritual strain of combat which lies ahead. Actually, however, I think the thoughts of all of us turn to the days of peace, and most of the emphasis in my preaching is on preparation for the task remaining after the war. One of the most difficult things to do is to convince men, against the natural reactions of fighters, and the efforts of the army, that they should not corrupt their souls with hatred. . . .

Like the western half of New Guinea, all of Indonesia had been a Dutch colony until it was invaded by the Japanese.

Sunday afternoon I went to the NICA (Netherlands Indies Civil Authority) compound for a church service, which was quite an experience. Gathered there are civil servants of the Dutch government who were detainees of the Japanese until liberated by our men. They have not yet returned to their former duties administering and policing the native populations. They are Javanese, Ambonese, Celebes, Malays, and some native Papuans: men, women, and many children. Most of them are Protestant Christians. Their Javanese pastor is Julius Fenandaber, small like Charlie Chaplain with a diminutive mustache and an abundance of dark hair. His costume was a triumph of conservation—the only civilian suit in these parts. Other men wore what cast-off clothing they could find: Japanese, American, or native sarongs. He was distinctive in a threadbare suit of rusty black with broad stripes, a frayed white shirt, and a tattered but defiantly red bow tie. Among people forever smiling their broad, infectious smiles, he retained the gravity appropriate to his calling, or perhaps natural to one who has drunk deeply of the tragedy in their lives. He stood at the door of the palm thatched "chapel" hastily constructed for the worship of God in this temporary camp, to welcome his flock—and myself, a stranger come to worship with them.

A group of us had been refused admittance to the compound by the Javanese MP, very nervous at the necessity forced upon him of trying to prevent American soldiers from trespassing, but politely insistent. For me, however, he would make an exception. Glimpsing my cross, he was confused, and hastened to the pastor for advice. The pastor, in turn, consulted the Dutch lieutenant at his headquarters and came back with permission to welcome me courteously. With him was a sergeant of the Netherlands Indies Army Medical Corps, a lithe man from Timor, lean and graceful with a head held high, flashing eyes, well-carved features, and the most expressive hands—long and eloquent when used with feeling in speech. This sergeant could speak a little English for my benefit, and he was scheduled to be the preacher of the afternoon. As a lay pastor during the difficult days of war, he had sought, wherever he was, to preach the gospel to men and women in need of spiritual food. . . .

In the little chapel there were split logs for seats and, at the front, a pulpit of unfinished lumber and a bench of bamboo for the preacher. There I was seated as an honored guest. . . . The women sat decorously on one side of the aisle, the men on the other, the children everywhere—in the aisles, on the seats, on the platform even. To look at them you would understand why the Master, to encourage worship, set a child in their midst that they might see in him the Kingdom of Heaven. Most of the children were light shades of ivory or café au lait, although some were dark, even mahogany. All had the lovely liquid eyes of gentle forest creatures, with shy and beautiful smiles. Scrubbed as clean as Sunday school scholars everywhere, they dressed in their Sunday best—skimpy, although somehow the mothers had managed to save or create little dresses for the girls, noteworthy in this land of few clothes.

The small Papuan boys and girls were neither so clean nor so well dressed as the Indonesians, and they sat more quietly—as visitors rather than members of the congregation. There were only a few of them, accompanied by a tall, stern, black man with bushy hair and a proud expression, who sat well to the rear, like an ebony statue, clad only in shorts. There were no Papuan women there.

Stroup noted features that would be of particular interest to his mother.

The Indonesian and Javanese women were gentle, doll-like creatures, some quite lovely. Some dressed in native costumes, with bright colors predominating: a wrapped skirt nearly to the ankles, above that a little jacket of some contrasting shade. A few had silk batiks, but most material was humbler stuff, well worn and faded from many washings. Their tiny feet were bare, their oval faces framed by smooth black hair drawn severely to a large knot in the back. I noticed differences between them and the non-Christian women one sometimes sees. The folk of the East Indies are mostly of Islam, and while it is a practice less rigorous than the harsh creed of the desert Arabs, it is nonetheless a faith that finds no place for women. These women, on the other hand, have looked into the face of Christ. They mirrored a serenity and poise that comes to those who need not fear or feel inferior, being honored mothers of children of God. . . . There was one old woman who was a benediction to the service. She sat, a little figure, yet monumental, on the front seat of honor, her due as a mother in Israel. She was dressed all in black and her face was the color of old ivory.

The service was simple with an emphasis on song. They sang hymns and chanted Psalms. Only the pastor had a hymnal, but they knew the words. If they didn't, the pastor would chant a line or two and they would sing it, and then again he would chant, and they would pick up the song. His leadership and the congregational singing flowed together without a break. I didn't recognize any tunes; they were haunting melodies in minor keys, of the East, not the West. Yet there were words I knew. One song repeated a phrase in verses and chorus, and when I was told that it meant "We are marching to Zion," I could catch the "Zion" when they sang it.

The service was in Malay, the universal language of the Southwest Pacific. This corruption of Arabic brought strange words into Christian worship. God, of course, was "Allah." But the hymns were not praise of the severe deity of Muhammad. This was Allah, the Father. They all sang; even the little tots playing on the dirt floor would take up the melody in chirping voices. These were a people far from home who had been prisoners of the Japanese. I thought of other people who could not sing the Lord's song in a strange land. These, however, were of the New Dispensation, who find a song at midnight in the prison that this world can sometimes be.

There were many brief prayers interspersed throughout the service. They stood to pray, as they did to sing, and the sound of the pastor's voice as he led them was resonant with earnestness. They sounded like good prayers that would reach God, coming as they did from the heart.

The sergeant was eloquent as a preacher. I didn't have to understand what he said to catch the authentic quality of good preaching. The evidence was in the expressions of his face, even more in his eloquent hands and voice, but most of all in the rapt attention of his hearers.

Only one old deacon—barefooted and in cast-off overalls, seated in the front—dozed during the sermon. He awoke to take up the collection with a little net sack fastened to a bamboo pole. How many "widow's mites" went into that bag! These were men and women, for years in virtual slavery, even now without visible means of support. After the service I sent the deacon out with his bag to the GIs who could not get into the compound but had that much, at least, of the service brought to them. They responded nobly with the amused generosity of Americans. I think it was a good day for the church treasury. With the copper coins of the people were mixed the opulent paper of our men.

The important part of the service was the sermon. Not understanding a word, I still grasped much of what the sergeant was saying. After the service he interpreted the sermon to me. He had spoken on a favorite passage of mine that gives us the assurance that nothing shall be able to separate us from the love of God which is in Christ Jesus our Lord. How can anyone understand the Bible or enter into the meaning of the gospel unless he has known suffering? "The fellowship of His suffering" is no idle phrase. These people understood. The face of the speaker was a mobile mask of tragedy as he reminded them of all that they had been through. His eyes held the horror of it. His dark hands groped for something in the air before him or clenched as though he felt the agony of life as something physically painful to himself. Then, like the sun from behind a cloud, his eyes would light up, his whole face would shine, and the long fingers of his hand would touch his heart. Again and again this was repeated. I felt at the time what, afterwards, I learned he had said.

He spoke of their loneliness as wanderers, a long, long way from home; of the distance in time and space that separated them from all that had been dear; his face was inexpressibly sad. Then the light would dawn and joy would return as he cried, "But we who have the Lord Jesus, there is no loneliness in our hearts." He told of the sufferings that they had been through, reminding them that under the Japanese (I caught the hardness in his tone as he said "Japanese") they had been no more than slaves like the children of Israel under taskmasters in Egypt. "But we who have the Lord Jesus, in our hearts we are free." He reminded them, who needed no reminder, of the months and years wherein they had suffered want, with not enough rice to give them strength or to take from them the gnawing pangs of hunger, so that the aged died and the children would not grow. "But we who have the Lord Jesus, we have no hunger in the heart." He touched on their sorrow, the sorrow of all people in a world at war, and on the tears that had so often filled their eyes—it was as if he sobbed afresh. But then that wonderful light would illumine his face and the hand would touch his heart again, "But we who have the Lord Jesus, in our hearts there is joy." He spoke of death, the death of friends and family members, the constant threat of death to them all. Led by his eloquence they again walked through the darkness of the valley of the shadow. And then the light dawned, "But we who have the Lord Jesus, in our hearts is eternity." . . .

It was a mean hut filled with a shabby crowd of poor brown people. But the glory of the Lord shone round about them. Their bare feet stood in the dust of the dirt floor, but their heads were lifted up to where the light of God could touch their faces. . . .

I went back the next day with some hymnals for them . . . and I shall go back again as I am able. It was good to find in this strange land a colony of Heaven. . . .

Russell

Stroup was eager to leave regimental headquarters as soon as the head-
quarters chaplain returned from leave. He complained of being separated
from the men, yet some were seeking him out.

Dearest family,

The Catholic chaplain returned today from Australia. Tomorrow I'm going to try to move up to the 1st Battalion. I can, now that he is back, and heaven knows I'd rather be there than at headquarters. This is the place to be if you don't want to do anything. The work is in the battalions where most of the men are.

Some of the men find their way down here, but they must have a reason—they don't just drop in. This afternoon three visitors took up most of my time. One is typical of what too many men face out here. His wife wrote some time ago asking for a divorce. He refused, and now she has written to say she is having a child—not his—and insisting that she have her legal freedom. What a thing to learn on the other side of the world! It crushes morale, especially since he still thinks he loves her.

A boy, Catholic by birth, came in to talk. He felt no peace, yet couldn't find what he wanted in Catholicism. I told him about our faith and that stimulated eager questions. Again and again he broke in with the cry, "That's just what I've wanted!" Together we found what he had been seeking, and he gave his heart to Christ anew. The boy said, "Chaplain, it's so good to know that God isn't a commanding officer and I don't have to go through channels to reach him but can, as you say, go as I would to my father—He is a father, isn't he?"

The third boy wanted to become a Christian and, if possible, join the Baptist Church back home. We arranged for that. None of these men (including two on other days) have felt this call before or gone to the other chaplains. I certainly haven't preached evangelistic sermons. I think it is something more subtle, some influence that attracts them to God through me.

Too many of the other chaplains, I think, try to be "one of the boys." The men like them personally but don't feel that they are spiritual guides who would be interested in their problems. The chaplains, in turn, don't realize that the men have such problems. . . .

I wrote an article on "The Peace of God in Asia" which I have sent to you. I think it is good and might be worth publishing. It was inspired in part by reading "Between Laughter and Tears" by Ling Yutang, a bitter indictment of English and American policies toward China. I'm trying to work out another one, "The Pacifist Peril to Peace," which outlines some of the mistakes we who are pacifists made after the last war, with suggestions on how to avoid the same mistakes after this one.

Russell

Neither of the articles mentioned has survived.

Tuesday, October 24, 1944

Dearest family,

I was delighted to get the *Harper's* article. It read well in print, and I really enjoyed it. The most interesting thing was the editorial comment where the magazine seemed to feel they had to explain the article. What in heaven's name are they so nervous about? Maybe I'm dense, but I couldn't see any dynamite in my offering. To compare me to Theodore Parker is a bit extravagant!

Harper's gave Stroup's article second billing among a dozen pieces but toward the back of the issue added an editorial comment:

> *When Russell C. Stroup—himself a chaplain in the armed forces overseas— warms to his subject there is a quality about his analysis of the church's remoteness from the affairs of daily life which reminds one of earlier days in American church history. His concept of a clergyman as "one who should grapple with evil and deal on intimate terms with the all too sordid lives of men and women" reminded us of Theodore Parker, the self-trained son of a Lexington farmer-mechanic, standing before the Ministerial Conference in Boston ninety-three years ago, after his refusal to obey the Fugitive Slave Law, and calmly saying: "I am not afraid of men, I can offend them . . . I have written my sermons with a pistol on my desk . . ." We've come a long way since then, and in the process, if Chaplain Stroup is to be believed, the clergy has apparently salved the itch in its trigger finger.*

The editors were insightful to associate Stroup with a history of Christian radicalism. They seemed to endorse his contention that modern clergy were complacent and distant. Nevertheless, he took offense that the editors would think that his article needed an apology, and he was probably offended as well by the image they projected of a "pistol-packing-parson." Stroup never carried a gun, even in situations more dangerous than those faced by the radical abolitionist Theodore Parker. His weapon was his typewriter.

Stroup's letter continues with mention of another essay that Cranston was marketing with difficulty. Although that essay sounds particularly interesting, it has not survived.

Don't got to too much trouble about the article concerning the army. I thought, oddly enough, that it was the best organized of my outpourings—taking sight, sound, and smell as subjects and developing them. . . .

Russell

Sunday, October 29, 1944

Dearest family,

I had fine services this morning and this evening—the latter is just over. Tonight one boy said to me, "Chaplain, does it matter how often a fellow goes to service? I do enjoy them so much that I don't want to miss any." I assured him that, as far as I was concerned, he couldn't overdo it. He replied, "Well, when I'm at the service I can forget about everything and imagine I'm home again."

Another boy, showing me a little book of prayers, said, "I take this out before I go to bed and read a prayer. I read it aloud because the other guys in my tent are kind of ashamed to pray themselves. When I finish they say 'Thanks, Joe' and I know that they are glad."

This morning a sergeant told me, "Chaplain, you don't know what your services have meant to me. What you say is so simple and yet means so much. I guess that's because I'm pretty simple myself and don't know much about religion. But I know what does me good, and there are lots of fellows that think like I do. You can see how the crowd grows at every service, and I can tell you there'll be a lot more coming."

A captain said how much he enjoyed the service and then added, "You don't get a chance to know what the men think, but those of us who read their letters know how many fine things they say about you when they write home."

All of this indicates that we are getting somewhere.

The chaplain we have been looking for arrived today, a Lt. Sharp, United Presbyterian from Illinois. Now, I imagine, Chaplain Steineger will become hospital chaplain. Chaplain Hearn, a Catholic, along with Sharp and myself, will be with the 1st Regiment. I'll be assigned the 1st and 2d Battalions, while living with the 1st, and Sharp will be with the 3d Battalion. Hearn will stay at headquarters as regimental chaplain.

Although four chaplains were now assigned to the 1st Infantry Regiment, Stroup maneuvered so that two-thirds of the units were placed directly under his pastoral care. In a typical infantry configuration, a Battalion consisted of one thousand to twelve hundred men; thus, the 1st Regiment comprised three thousand or more men. The challenge of these chaplaincy assignments will become apparent when the units enter combat.

I've got an electric light in my tent so I can sit here at night and write. The only trouble is that it attracts a myriad of insects, all sorts. Finally they get so bad that I have to turn off the light and take refuge under the mosquito net that covers my cot. Fortunately, among the many insects there are few mosquitoes because we are at the edge of the ocean and the wind from the sea blows them inland. . . .

I have had two more men accept Christ, which makes five in two weeks. This will continue, I think, while I am with a group long enough to get to know them, and they to know me—until we are in the midst of combat when there is little opportunity for the personal work necessary. I have a sense of accomplishment. I receive a splendid response and feel that I can do great things. Everyone is *so* appreciative of all that I try to do. I shall be happy here.

Russell

Friday, November 3, 1944

Dearest family,

The next several weeks I will be working with the men, and getting acquainted with them, preparatory to the tougher experiences ahead. These experiences are relatively brief—not more than a couple of months—but difficult while they last.

I have been enjoying myself by writing a very fierce article on "The Gospel Gestapo"—a delicious title—that exposes [certain fundamentalist preachers of note at the time]. Everyone seems afraid to tackle those babies or to bring their activities into the open. I get a lot of fun doing it, even though what I write might never be published. I wish it might. Socrates said he was the gadfly of the state, and I sometimes have ambitions to be the gadfly of the Church—if such a fly could awaken it out of the profound slumber it now enjoys. God says that we should have no graven images, yet the Church sets up so many that it needs iconoclasts to smash them. It also needs men of creative power to build. I really ought to concentrate on the constructive end, but it isn't as much fun. And I need a safety valve to work off pent-up steam that accumulates in the army. I find release in attacking the follies of the Church since I can't write about the follies of the army.

Come to think of it, I just realized the truth in the hymn phrase, "Like a mighty army moves the church of God." I had always taken this as a compliment to the Church. Now I realize that it is quite the contrary—yet only too true of the confusion, cross purposes, lack of unity, blundering stupidity, as well as the sacrificial glory of the Church.

Some GI linemen are stringing wires near my tent, fastening them on tall poles that they have erected. Rather, I should say, they ought to be fastening them, but with the delightful ingenuity of Americans they have persuaded little native boys to do this for them. These kids with their marvelous feet and hands go up a pole faster and easier than linemen with their steel climbing spikes. The kids seem to enjoy it too, so everyone is satisfied. I marvel at how well the soldiers and the natives get along and make themselves understood when neither knows a word of the other's language—except "OK," which is basic to all.

We have had gales lately blowing in off the ocean and I have spent a couple of nights hanging on to my tent lest it blow away and leave me even more exposed to the elements than I was which was plenty with the rain soaking through the canvas and blowing in great gusts through the openings. The wind starts blowing and then off in the distance you can hear the rain coming nearer and nearer like Niagara Falls on wheels until all of a sudden it hits you with a bang. How it can pour!

I get much more work done now that I am away from regimental headquarters—and the other chaplains—and out here on my own with the battalion. It embarrassed me to do much that I wanted to do around the other chaplains since it seemed to reflect on their inactivity. It can still be embarrassing. The other battalion chaplain asked me this morning how many men were at my service last night. I didn't reply but asked my assistant and he said, "About one hundred and twenty." I didn't dare say it myself knowing how unbelievable it would be. The chaplain looked his astonishment and blurted out, "A hundred and twenty! I had SIX!" I'm not particularly proud of 120 men for a midweek service out of the thousand men I have to serve—but SIX? Ye gods, what a tragic waste and, dear God, what a lost opportunity. I fear they think that I take their men, for this past week they decided not to post announcements about who would be preaching where.

Russell

Monday, November 6, 1944

Dearest family,

We had a very good day on Sunday. I preached in an Air Corps chapel since the chaplain there was on leave. They had a good crowd out, one of the best I've seen outside of my own unit. Attendance at my unit held its own despite competition from a championship ball game scheduled at the same time. The evening communion service was also well attended. Tomorrow I go by boat to hold a service with an outlying unit. That evening there will be a Tuesday discussion group which I have inaugurated in my unit and which shows great promise. Then on Thursday our midweek service, which is really becoming quite phenomenal.

I have sent to Cranston two more articles that are really meant to be chapters in my book, if it ever materializes. They might have other uses. I'm going to keep on batting them out as I can. It gives me some mental exercise and can't do any harm.

Russell

Wednesday, November 8, 1944

Dearest family,

The first election news came to us this evening by radio. We were watching movies when they announced that while Dewey had not yet conceded the election it seemed a foregone conclusion that Roosevelt was elected. There was much applause from the crowd. The joy, of course, was not unanimous. For myself, while I am not sorry to have Dewey defeated and the Democrats still in office, I do hate to have a president begin a fourth term. I hope that he proves himself worthy of this trust, but I am fearful of one who was never a humble man. Success and power are heady drinks that befuddle the minds of men. We shall need clear thinking and a willingness to be guided by a wisdom not our own.

I am haunted by a vision—not of a confident man leaning back with a cigarette holder pointed skyward from a smiling face—but of a tragic figure in ancient black who wore a stovepipe hat and a faded shawl over his shoulders, bent with the burdens of humanity. He had the sign of the cross in his eyes. "With malice toward none," he said, "with charity toward all; with firmness in the right as God gives us to see the right, let us bind up the nation's wounds. . . ."

But I rejoice with you tonight even at this distance. I can see Mother's confident smile and hear Cranston's exultation. I wish I were there to share it with you. I fear I'll have to wait a long time for another such opportunity, for surely 1948 will be a Republican year. . . .

Cranston had sold a few more of Stroup's words.

Imagine, getting $50 from the *Ladies' Home Journal* for a paragraph. The trouble is that one can't sell many paragraphs. I'm getting greedy for fame and fortune. . . .

Russell

7

"Men Would See Jesus"

Dearest family,

I have been puzzling over the Christmas message that I would like to put on our family cards or in the church bulletin. It isn't easy to find just the right thing to say. The following almost scans, although it is prose and not poetry.

Give God good thanks this Christmas-tide Who has given us to hear above the noise of bitter strife the Angels' Song of Peace. The hearts within us all rejoice for the hope which they proclaim of a New Year blessed with Victory and our return to Home.

So let us then to Bethlehem with burning Faith to find the Christ Whose Love within our hearts can give to all mankind a New Year bright with promise and a New World blessed with Peace.

I think this expresses, albeit a bit impersonally, the message that I would like to send this particular Christmas.

The past two nights we have had a return engagement from Tojo with planes coming over but doing little damage. I should have thought they would be much too busy elsewhere to bother with us, but I try to appreciate the implied compliment. Fortunately I didn't even wake up either time and only learned about it in the morning from those who did. I must be thoroughly acclimated to aerial bombardment. There was a time when I would have been alert even before the radar. . . .

Golly, what a rain! It is almost too dark to see so I think I'll bring this to a close. With all my love to you,

Russell

Dearest family,

Two good services this morning and two fine letters this afternoon put me in an excellent mood—except for intestinal disturbances due to today's dietary abominations. We have been having pork, pork, and more pork. The poor mess sergeants try to doctor it up but it still comes out pork whether it is sausage or wieners or Spam.

I went to the Air Corps as I did last Sunday and the large chapel they have was filled, with men standing up in the rear and around the sides. Last week the men were enthusiastic about the message and asked me to return so long as their chaplain is away.

My own service had an even larger crowd, which is to be expected, and for the first time a new battalion commander of the 2d Battalion was there, together with the regimental commander who has been with us before. In fact, although they have a chapel service at regimental headquarters, he comes down for my service, by preference I guess.

Before the Air Force service I received a man into the Church as a result of last week's service. After our battalion service two men came to see me and will join later.

Then there was a lad this afternoon, a pathetic man of thirty, who was raised in an orphan asylum of the worst type where he learned nothing useful. He became a hobo traveling throughout the country. He felt his life was a failure and hoped that, in the army, he might feel useful. But here it was the same story and he was licked. There was no one who cared about him, no one who wrote to him, no one to whom it mattered whether he lived or died. He stayed with me over two hours and will be back again. I hope I helped him. He felt some stirrings of hope and said, "One bad thing about feeling this way is that, up until now I didn't care whether I was killed or not, and now I think I want to live so I can begin life all over again." Considering our prospects, perhaps I did him more harm than good. . . .

There will be another service tonight. Already some of the men have stopped by to ask me about it: two just left. I like the evening service, for it comes just when the sunset over the water is so beautiful. I think of Jacob's exclamation, "This is the house of the Lord. This is none other than the gate of heaven!" . . .

I have just returned from that service. My description was inadequate. The sunset was glorious, and the service wasn't bad. A sergeant said afterwards, "That's the best sermon I ever heard." . . .

There are a lot of things about the international situation that I don't understand, and they worry me. I suspect that the English are too slick for us, and the Russians too ruthless. Yet we have to work with them. The best policy for America would be to refuse to play either of their games, to insist on an idealism that is wholly unselfish—as we can afford to be—and to back up our insistence with our power and prestige. If we could free the world, rather than rule the world, that world might be less dangerous to us and to others. I wish with all my heart that Henry Wallace were closer to the inner councils of the president and could have more to do with the framing of peace.

Russell

When "A Soldier Looks at the Church" was published in Harper's *it created a stir, and news about the essay appeared in other journals as well.*

Friday, November 17, 1944

Dearest family,

I received Mother's letter containing the *Christian Science Monitor* clipping and the one from *Newsweek.* I wonder where *Newsweek* got its description of me as a "shy 39-year-old bachelor." It sounds like advertising. I can't figure out whether they think I am shy because I am thirty-nine and a bachelor, or a bachelor at thirty-nine because I am shy.

The whole *Newsweek* magazine has also arrived in these parts and caused considerable comment among my friends. Of course I'm going to suffer for some time from that "shy" statement.

I'm glad you like the article about our policy in the Far East ["The Peace of God in Asia"]. Cranston is a good agent, and I think I can trust him to place it. Even if he tries unsuccessfully with the more important journals, it will eventually reach its proper level. I hope he gets a kick out of representing me in this capacity. It is easier for me to have him get the rejection slips than to get them myself. I miss all the grief and reap all the profit. . . .

There is considerable speculation here as to whether or not we shall have turkey for Thanksgiving, and the bulk of opinion is that we won't, which pessimism I share. I'd settle for any kind of fresh meat. We have been having the poorest menus it has been my misfortune to eat. . . .

Another lad accepted Christ after my service Thursday. He's been so happy about it since that I can hardly turn around without finding him underfoot waiting to tell me all about it for the one hundredth time. I pity the boys who live in his tent. They were foolish enough to comment on how changed he seemed. That gave him an opportunity to tell all about it—but I won't add you to his audience.

Russell

Tuesday, November 21, 1944

Dearest family,

Thank you for interesting articles concerning the late election. Now I can rest content for another four years when it will be my pleasure to oppose a fifth term for Roosevelt. You asked if I voted this time and I am forced to say I did not. My ballot went to my old outfit and I'll get it sometime, but too late to be any good. I'm just as glad, though, for I couldn't in conscience have voted for Dewey and I doubt if I could have brought myself to help elect a man to a fourth term, even Roosevelt.

I have received two letters commenting on an editorial about me in the *Christian Century,* but nobody has sent me the editorial. The fact that they have devoted an editorial to my article should encourage them to look with favor on other writing of mine that you might send to them. Don't scorn the *Christian Century,* Cranston. They have more influence than any other religious paper, I think. Also, they pay.

I enclose a little thing I wrote about Heaven, just to get down the thoughts. There are some things I don't know about the subject, but I am not alone in that. For the present I'm content to picture it in my imagination. Yet I think the subject needs some exploration.

Russell

Thanksgiving Day, November 23, 1944

Dearest family,

You have been much on my mind and in my heart today. I think the whole Regiment was AWOL in spirit today, our minds having sneaked off to the far-flung firesides where we sat down to delectable feasts with folks back home.

Everything was done here to make the day as good as it could be. The morning was not busy, and we all had the afternoon off. The Thanksgiving Day service engaged my attention. I enclose the program. We had a splendid attendance and I think that the service gave the men a feeling of home and real Thanksgiving.

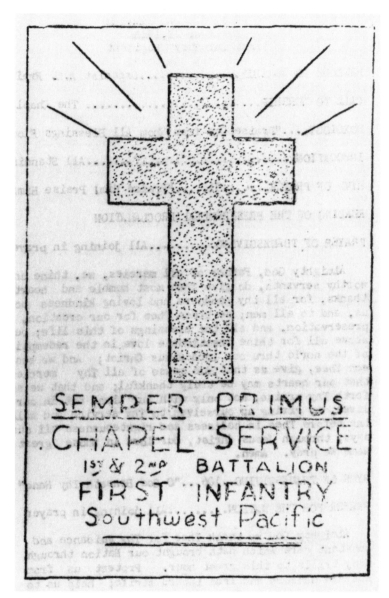

The Thanksgiving Day Service bulletin shows that worship for the 1st and 2d Battalions was combined under Stroup's leadership. The 3d Battalion was served by another Protestant chaplain.

THANKSGIVING DAY SERVICE
November 23,1944
First Infantry Regiment

PRELUDE TO WORSHIP..............Organist R.W. Freitag.

CALL TO WORSHIP.................... The Chaplain

DOXOLOGY...."Praise God from Whom All Blessings Flow:"

INVOCATION.............................All Standing

HYMN OF PRAISE.......91....."Praise Him! Praise Him!"

READING OF THE PRESIDENTIAL PROCLAMATION

PRAYER OF THANKSGIVING...........All joining in prayer

   Almighty God, Father of all mercies, we, thine un-
worthy servants, do give Thee most humble and hearty
thanks, for all thy goodness and loving kindness to
us, and to all men; we bless Thee for our creation,
preservation, and all the blessings of this life; but
above all for thine inestimable love in the redemption
of the world thru our Lord Jesus Christ; And we bese-
ech Thee, give us that due sense of all Thy mercies,
that our hearts may be truly thankful; and that we show
forth Thy praise, not only with our lips, but in our
lives, by giving up ourselves to Thy service and walking before Thee in holiness and righteousness all our
days; through Jesus Christ, Our Lord in Whose great
Name we pray. Amen.

HYMN OF THANKSGIVING..106..."O God Beneath Thy Hand"

PRAYER FOR THE NATION...........All joining in prayer

   Almighty God we thank Thee for Thy guidance and
constant care which hath brought our Nation through
many trials to this great hour. Protect us from
outward dangers and from inward strife; help us to

Stroup favored a simple liturgy, yet the wording of the prayers was lofty and
traditional. The Scripture reading and the sermon provided the climax.

maintain an honorable place among the nations and
give us the opportunity of increasing service to
the world. Make us strong and great in the fear
of God, and in the love of righteousness; so that,
being blessed of Thee, we may become a blessing to
all nations; to the praise of the glory of Thy
grace; through Jesus Christ our Lord. Amen.

QUARTET..."Come Ye Thankful People".....R. Freitag
                                          H. Gave
                                    C. Gilbert
                                  T. Williamsen

SCRIPTURE READING........Deuteronomy Chapter VIII

THANKSGIVING DAY MESSAGE...Chaplain Russell Stroup

HYMN OF AMERICA...144..."My Country 'tis of Thee"

BENEDICTION..................All remain standing

MOMENT OF SILENT MEDITATION.............POSTLUDE

        ....*********..

    On Special Days like Thanksgiving we all re-
member in special ways our homes and families;
our friends and firesides. Separated by many
miles they are very close to our hearts, to-day,
and we thank God for the remembrance of them and
pray God that the time will not be distant when
we shall see them again. Meanwhile let us write
home to-day, and send this program when we do.

             REMEMBER OUR SERVICES

Sunday Morning Worship Service at 1000 in the Theatre
Sunday Evening Song Service at 1800 in the Theatre
Tuesday Evening Disscussion Group at 1800, Ch. Tent
Mid-week Service, Thursday, 1800 in the Theatre.

*The note following the service urged soldiers, when they wrote home, to send
this bulletin to their families.*

.FIRST INFANTRY REGIMENT .
SCHEDULE OF PROTESTANT SERVICES
1st and 2nd Battalions

****

SUNDAY

Morning Worship Service............... 1000
Vesper Service 1800
Holy Communion First Sunday of each Month

WEEKDAY

Discussion Group ...Tuesday 1800
Chaplain's Tent
Song and Prayer Service.. Thursday... 1800
in the Theatre

****

CONSULTATION HOURS
The Chaplain is always in his tent during your free
hours, daily from 1100-1130 hours, 1500-1700 hours
and 2030-2130 hours, or at any other time by previous
arrangement. Come and see him any time for any reason.

CAPTAIN RUSSELL C. STROUP................CHAPLAIN
T/5 Thomas Williamsen....................Assistant

*In addition to conducting the three weekly services and the discussion group,
Stroup advertised his availability during each of the three free periods that
soldiers enjoyed during the day. The last line introduces Thomas Williamsen, the
chaplain's assistant. The regimental command, appreciating Stroup's tendency
to expose himself to danger, gave Williamsen orders to never let the chaplain
out of his sight.*

The big moment was the noon meal. The government got a plentiful supply of frozen turkeys to us—whole birds, just as they would be at home. Each company of about 150 to 200 men had about 200 pounds of turkey. Since the turkeys had to be cooked on just two field ranges in each company, cooking began the night before and continued through the morning. There was fruit cocktail from cans, mashed potatoes, dressing, peas, pickles, cranberry sauce, fresh rolls, pumpkin pie, and coffee. Plenty of everything filled every nook and cranny of the men. They left the groaning boards as stuffed as the turkeys had been, to lay around for a sunlit afternoon. By supper we were back to bully beef, but no one cared since no one was hungry yet.

I had invitations from many messes to have turkey dinner with them. I appreciate the fact that they wanted me, especially as each extra person reduced the amount of precious bird for the others. I ate with C Company, which is right next door to my tent, although I am supposed to mess at headquarters.

Russell

Sunday, November 26, 1944

Dearest family,

It is almost too hot to write, with very little breeze, but I've taken off my shirt and turned back the flap of the tent to catch what moving air there may be. I will make a try even though the typewriter is hot to the touch and my hands are sweaty on the keys. In all the stories, South Sea "planters" sit on shaded, screened verandas with tall, frosty drinks at hand. No such delights are reserved for us, save that I sit. Considering that this is the middle of the summer season, the heat is not surprising and—"tell it not in Gath"—there have been many days no less oppressive in Lynchburg, Va.

Last night I saw Noel Coward's movie *In Which We Serve*, an old film telling the story of a British destroyer, and telling it very well. But for the first time out here I saw most of the audience get up and leave. I've left several times when the show was some truly awful product, but this was good. Of course, it concerned the war, which they don't like to see, and it was filled with patriotic sentiment, which is anathema. This isn't just a lack of patriotic fervor: it's actual hatred of anything that suggests it. They fall for all sorts of cheap sentiment, except that one. I think that underneath they do have a feeling for their country, but they refuse to let on. Compared with every other army, we have done a poor job of indoctrination. This may be just as well, but personally I still have in me a good deal of the old screaming-eagle Americanism.

A boy visited me with a letter from his wife, who insisted, in a pathetic and apparently sincere letter, that she did love him, but that in a moment of weakness made up of loneliness and boredom she had slipped badly and was going to have a baby—not his. We had a long talk. He was angry and hurt and talked wildly. At last, though, I persuaded him to write to her that he would go right on helping her in every way until the baby came, and that neither she nor the baby would suffer. He also agreed that the baby could have his name: at first he violently objected, but I tried to show him how innocent the child was. Finally he said, "You know, that little fellow is just like me. We both have to suffer for what isn't our fault." Then, more fiercely, "I ain't going to allow that kid to suffer any!" This was big of him, and wise. Later, he showed me his letter and it was a good one.

There are going to be lots of problems when the boys come home, and I have a world of sympathy for them and for the girls back there. I tried to help him see what his wife's life must have been with him away. War is a mess any way you look at it, and the by-products are worse than the direct consequences. No good can come out of such iniquity.

The service was good this morning. I'm going to have to get a public address system, for the crowd is too large for me to reach them—all out-of-doors as we are—without straining my voice. This is the first time I have had that trouble.

Russell

Wednesday, November 29, 1944

Dearest Cran,

It was grand to get your long letter, and I want to answer in some detail if the boys will give me the time and not bother me too much with their problems. But it is the time of day when I expect them.

Your plans for the articles suit me. You have more experience and more knowledge than I have. Just don't scorn Mother's suggestions, for her business eye is more shrewd than either of ours.

It isn't easy to write out here. I don't have the time and, more important, I don't have necessary freedom from distraction, nor do I have conversation with like-minded people and books to read. Any well will go dry, or get a bit brackish, if there is no water flowing in. My intellectual water supply doesn't get much replenishing. The thoughts of the average American male are not pearls of great price, and out here they are even less so.

When I get home I want to arrange life so I get three months off each summer during the slack season. In such time I could do some really creative writing. Overall, I would like to devote 25 percent of my time to writing, 25 percent to general speaking, and 50 percent to the Church. That could give me a living and an opportunity to spread myself more broadly.

Radio is the big opportunity for moneymaking, and I have a voice for that. A little publicity gained from articles published before I get home, plus a voice test afterwards, could produce some opening in that field. With radio one can be anywhere—Lynchburg or New York—for a national hookup. . . .

We decided Sunday to install a loudspeaker system for our services, as the crowd is getting too large. However, when I think of the crowd that turned out last Sunday night for a show by an all-GI group, and appreciate the pitiful quality of that performance, I cannot be conceited about the considerably smaller number that came to hear me in the morning. However, it is many times the number that they were accustomed to.

Russell

Friday, December 1, 1944

Dearest family,

It might be interesting for me to detail the events of one of my ordinary days—yesterday. I am called to consciousness by the sound of a bugle blowing first call, and I lie here adjusting myself to a new day, and offering a prayer to God for the day. I can hear the sound of the sea and the noises of men as the camp comes awake. It is six o'clock. In a moment reveille will blow and I'll pile out of my cot, pushing aside the mosquito bar and sitting sleepily on the edge. I pull on my clothes as rapidly as possible, for time is limited. I gather my toilet articles and my steel helmet, fill the latter with water from a can, and proceed with ablutions that include a hasty shave. By this time chow call has sounded, and I am off to the mess—there to partake of Cream of Wheat, toast and jam, and coffee. I pass by the dehydrated scrambled eggs, not having developed a taste for them. Then I go back to my tent to make up my cot, put away my things, and be ready for half an hour of calisthenics at seven-thirty.

By eight I am mapping out the day's work with my assistant while I wait for the jeep to take me to the division headquarters for a meeting of all chaplains at nine o'clock. We gather to discuss work for the next three months—pretty important. We receive detailed instructions along with advice and warnings. Supplies for the period, such as Testaments, communion elements, etc., are passed out. Then we adjourn to the open for a group picture. There are fifteen chaplains in the division as well as others from units attached to the task force.

Back at my tent I have an hour to work on a monthly report that must be turned in that day. Working rapidly, I finish it by eleven, for I know that men will then begin to drift in to see me. Eleven to eleven-thirty is the time when everyone is supposed to take a swim in the ocean, but many seize the opportunity to call on me with their problems. Only two men called this morning, so I had a chance to think about the worship for this evening.

Eleven-thirty is chow time. The menu is bully beef, dehydrated potatoes, canned creamed asparagus, bread and what passes for butter, a type of pudding that looks and tastes like wallpaper paste, and cold cocoa. Not caring for the rest, I eat asparagus on bread and drink cocoa, which is enough for my lunch.

From noon to one we are supposed to lie down and rest, but I take time to read the daily news on four mimeographed sheets—fairly complete. Then I lie down. Yesterday I was able to fall asleep, which I don't usually do, but alas I was awakened by some lad who had enough troubles to keep me occupied until one o'clock.

At one I went down to the personnel office to get my pay, the most of which ($125) I turned back to them to send on to you. I then called on the special service officer to discuss problems relating to entertainment, reading, etc. On the walk back to my tent I stopped here and there to talk with groups of men engaged in various training activities. They fire rifles, mortars, and machine guns out to sea, and as I walk along the shore I can pass the time of day with them.

It is almost three o'clock when I get back, knowing that at three-thirty the men will be off work, or rather engaged in athletics and swimming. I take time to doctor my feet for jungle rot, then sit down to wait for the inevitable callers. They do come: yesterday there were four between three-thirty and four-thirty.

I knock off for a quick dip in the ocean and an open-air shower, and dress in clean khakis. I'm ready for retreat, which we stand at five-ten. For most men this means inspection of rifles, etc., but for me it means simply to be there and to stand at attention while retreat is blown and the flag is lowered.

Five-thirty is chow. We have what we have had so often lately: chili, macaroni, spinach, bread, pears, and coffee. I pass up the chili but eat the rest, and hasten to my service at six.

There is a good crowd gathered in the open-air theater, perhaps a hundred and fifty men, while the sun sets in glory off to our right. We sing songs of their choice, including "Leaning on the Everlasting Arms," " 'Tis So Sweet to Trust in Jesus," "God Will Take Care of You," "Since Jesus Came into My Heart," "Count Your Many Blessings," "Have Thine Own Way Lord," and others. Then, when it is too dark to sing anymore, I give them a message of courage and confidence, using the story of Paul and Silas in the Philippian jail. By six-forty-five the service is over.

Since a Tuesday entertainment by GIs had made our discussion group impossible, a lot of the men asked to have it on Thursday after our service. They came to my tent from seven until nine. I have three long benches in the tent where they can sit, as well as on my cot, while I use the one chair. We talked about anything relating to our religious life. This is always stimulating.

From nine until ten I did some reading and then decided to go to bed. It was raining by then, and since the tent leaks I spread a poncho over the top of my mosquito bar frame and crawled beneath it. It was too hot for covers, but I dropped off to sleep. I awakened about one o'clock to draw a blanket over me and then fell asleep once more. The bugle awakened me at four-thirty this morning, since we were all going out to the range and wanted to get the shooting over with before it got too hot in that exposed place. So endeth one day in my life, more or less typical of them all.

Russell

Monday, December 4, 1944

Dearest family,

This is written on stationery contained in the box sent out by the First Presbyterian Church of Lynchburg, Virginia, to their boys in the service. It is very nice: the first Christmas present I have received. All of the men have been getting presents, and there is quite a festive atmosphere about the place. I think no one is waiting to open them. If something comes from you, however, I'll keep it for a while. I wouldn't say anything to anyone in the church about my opening theirs. I couldn't resist the temptation, with other boxes being opened around me. Anyhow, this is St. Nicholas eve; for the Dutch that's Christmas Eve; when in Rome do as the Romans do! They are having Christmas for the children at the NICA compound tomorrow and I hope to be there to help them celebrate. The soldiers have gotten together a lot of gifts for them, with Santa Claus and all—not the soldiers I am with but those near the compound. They asked me to come over, and I'm eager to visit.

In case you don't know, the boxes from the church are very nice, most attractively packed, with a well-thought-out selection. There is stationery and envelopes and air-mail stamps—all of them mighty useful out here. There are two books: one by Somerset Maugham and one of verse. There's a box of lead pencils, another scarce item in these parts. There is a copy of *Time* and of the *Saturday Evening Post;* and finally a copy of the *Lynchburg Advance* containing an editorial about my [*Harper's*] article. . . .

The issue of *Newsweek* featuring me has just hit the camp, and I am quite a celebrity. It was difficult for many to believe that I was the guy it was talking about, which is no compliment. I guess they don't expect chaplains to be any great shakes.

I am finishing up an article on pacifism which is not as polished as I would like, but I had best get it done and off to you. . . .

We had two grand services yesterday: the largest crowd yet at both the morning service and the communion service in the evening. At the latter, I thought the men would never stop coming forward. The service was brief, and I had no sermon, but we were over an hour serving the men. Most of the service was in the dark except for the light of candles. It was most impressive to see a long line of men kneeling, and then another take their place, and another, and another. There are many things that make it worth while to be here. I think these are services which the men will not forget.

Russell

P.S. I finally sent a souvenir from the 41st Infantry Division—a genuine hari-kari knife. I hope it reaches you, but it is a rather tempting thing for someone to lift. [In a subsequent letter to Cranston, Stroup added the following.] It was found in one of the many caves which made our operation so costly. As you will see it suffered somewhat from its experiences but can be made alright. . . . An aviator offered me $250 for it. It certainly isn't worth that to me. Under the circumstances of its use I could hardly sell it, but the temptation was great.

Dearest family,

. . . Don't worry too much about the climate out here. It really isn't as bad as it seems from accounts. . . . Anyhow, we won't be in New Guinea forever, and the climate here is the worst. I got rid of the fungus growth on my face before I got to Australia, and haven't had a return. I've not been so lucky with my feet, but the rest of my body is free of fungus. . . .

I'm glad that you like the two articles I mailed home. I think you are probably right about their publication. Especially the "Gospel Gestapo." There is no use rubbing it in, and I don't want to get a reputation as a chronic critic. . . . As for the one on liturgy: the very persons who wouldn't agree with the other article might like that one. Most of the conservative members of the churches in the south are opposed to excessive ritual. It is the progressives who favor it. So that article might serve as a counterirritant. At least I don't think it would do much harm. We can let the Gestapo age in the wood for a while. I write not to get them published but to get them home where I'll have them safe. . . . I would like to write something really constructive. That is what I thought about "The Peace of God in Asia." It tended to exalt the church where my other article tended to attack it. . . . I have no desire to be foolhardy, but neither am I inclined to be overly cautious. Being here in the presence of death keeps one from worrying about petty annoyances. . . .

Stroup preferred simple worship centered in Scripture and sermon. He associated elaborate liturgy with insincerity. When his article on liturgy was published a year later in the Presbyterian Outlook *under the title "The Fatal Lure of Liturgy," it stirred more controversy than any of the eight articles by him that preceded it in that magazine. Those eight, however, had been rooted in his South Pacific experiences, while the liturgy diatribe was not.*

The history of the regiment which I wrote has just been published with one copy for each man. The colonel talked to me about it this morning, as have many others who think it very fine, although in the publication I'm given no credit for writing. However, both the general of the division and the general of the corps have commended me. . . .

We are now planning for our Christmas entertainment. I made an announcement this morning, asking for men to form a chorus to sing Christmas songs on Christmas Eve. After the service a navy lieutenant, who is stationed with us, said that he was trained to be a choir director and would like to take that over. He will, and I think that ought to help. . . .

The services today were fine with a splendid attendance at both. We are now having as many in the evenings as we did in the morning services when I first arrived. And the morning services are really remarkable. I didn't think it was possible to have so many out. We almost fill the theater—well, not quite, but we have a mighty good crowd in an awfully big theater made to accommodate the whole regiment. . . .

I'll try to answer as many of the letters in my fan mail as I have addresses. They deserve some recognition besides *Harper's* form letters. I'll do my best. Thanks for these letters, and for everything. Loads of love,

Russell

Friday, December 15, 1944

Dearest family,

I've been wondering and worrying about the question of what the American soldier thinks he is fighting for in this war. I have been tempted to agree with Jack Belden, who wrote in his book *Still Time to Die* that "our men do not believe they are fighting for anything. Not one in a hundred has any deep-seated political belief." Yet I come back to the fact that men do not fight courageously, suffer patiently, or die heroically—as these men certainly do—without something to sustain them, some inner convictions which strengthen their souls.

They don't talk about it. They scoff at the patriotic sentiments that were so familiar to us of another generation. . . . The songs they sing are not martial but maudlin. They seek no glory and they find none in battle. The super-patriotism of the Nazi, the Japanese, or the Russian leaves these men cold. The simplest sort of appeal to a nationalistic spirit is dismissed as "propaganda for the home front." Let the hero in a Hollywood spectacle talk of his eagerness to die for the Four Freedoms and they will walk out on the show. Yet behind this seeming cynicism and disillusionment there must lie something waiting to be found. I think I have a hint of what it may be.

You have seen the cartoons "Out Front with Mauldin." They are a favorite with soldiers everywhere. The cartoons, and their leading character Joe, seem to epitomize the very lack of which I have been speaking. But something was revealed to me by Mauldin's assertion that Joe "is just the average U.S. combat soldier, leading a life he hates so bitterly that he is fighting a war to get it over with." In that "hatred" is contained all the convictions that are American—and some hope for a new world.

The American soldier hates the life he is living because he hates militarism. He wants no part of it. There is hope for humanity in that holy hatred. The gray columns "Under der Linden" or in Red Square, with the crowds that cheer them on, are the calamity of our times. There is none of that in the American army. These are not soldiers, our men, but civilians in uniform. They are the heirs of a great tradition, peculiarly American, of men who took down a long rifle from above the mantel and went out to protect their homes.

Conquering legions are not made up of such stuff. The peace of the world will never be disturbed, but always restored, by such men. They will dethrone and destroy the sawdust Caesars, and defeat and disarm their goose-stepping followers, but they will not take up arms themselves unless they are driven to it by the grim necessity of unprovoked attack. The world is safe in their hands, for those hands are at home with tools, not weapons. They are builders and not destroyers. They are citizens, not soldiers. In other words they are Americans: fighting as Americans have always fought—against militarism, which has no place in our way of life.

You cannot regiment Americans. The hatred by our GIs for the life they are forced to live is proof of that. . . . The soldier knows that in the army this is necessary, but he doesn't like it any better for that. He has a distinctly American distaste for uniforms. It embarrasses him to wear one. He resents the fact that he must. That is really the secret of it: he will put a uniform on for his lodge back home, but that is his choice; it is one of many things which he may wear. Your American likes variety and he likes to wear what he pleases, when he pleases, and to take it off if he pleases.

There are a lot of men in the army who are eating better now than they ever did at home, but they don't like it. They don't like it because they are forced to eat it. They would rather have less, like home, but have it when they want it and how they want it. The more I see of the soldier, the more convinced I am that he will never be willing to purchase economic improvement at the price of regimentation. . . .

There is something about the American that doesn't like authority. . . . He may like his officer as a man, but he hates him as an authority. He does a job willingly only when he is asked, never when he is ordered—even if he knows the job is for his own benefit. We are an undisciplined lot, which is bad, but I am convinced that discipline for Americans must be self-discipline. It can never be imposed upon us by authority from without. You can plan all you want for universal military training, but you will never persuade our people that they like that kind of business. They will fight for the right to do as they please and be let alone. That is something they are fighting for now, and I think it is a good thing.

They hate the life they are living because they are under authority, discipline, and regimentation, but they will accept it as a means to secure the future in which they will be free from all such restraint. In other words, they are fighting for freedom.

The American soldier hates the life he is living because it involves discomfort. It isn't that he can't take it. He has proved that he can, but he doesn't like it. He wants a world in which he can be comfortable. He wants a world in which he can have the security, and even luxury, denied him in the army, and he thinks he is entitled to it. I think he is too, and I think he is going to get it. He is sold on the idea of abundance, and he intends to have it. That is something he is fighting for. It may be purely material, but it is all bound up with the problem of a more abundant life for mankind.

The American soldier hates the life he is living because he is tempted to hate and forced to destroy, when he likes to be friendly and to build. . . . In spite of any official discouragement, he will fraternize with prisoners and conquered peoples. It is in his blood. We are the friendliest people in the world. In spite of the plague spots of prejudice in our national life, fundamentally we are eager to get along with everyone and be friends to all. There is hope for the future in that. I do not believe that you can make good haters out of Americans. . . . The solution to ills of humanity is bound up in this spirit of friendliness which is so characteristically American. We are fighting for that. . . .

Russell

At home, Cranston chafed under the physical and neurological limitations of encephalitis. At times his shaking hands could not hold objects; his mind would be sharp, then cloudy; his moods changed without warning. He resented the impact of the disease on his health, his strength, and his search for romance. He missed his brother and wished to join him. While both Cranston and his mother warned Stroup to be more careful, Cranston hoped that the army might honor his brother with a Bronze or Silver Star for bravery. Stroup tried, not always successfully, to respond to his older brother without patronizing him.

Tuesday, December 19, 1944

Dearest Cran,

. . . I have not the slightest chance of getting the star now, I fear, for I have heard nothing from the 41st [Infantry Division] beyond what I have told you. Do not imagine for a moment that I shall ever be guilty of going in search of one. I would never risk so much for so little, a ribbon to stick on my coat. Uh uh. Not me. My one desire is to do my job without heroics and to get safely home where I have work waiting and folks to love. . . .

I think it will more likely be the dog days than the dogwood before I see you again. There is a little business to transact first and that takes a little time. I doubt if I will be free much before Allan's birthday [April 1]. . . .

I had a lovely letter from Peggy [a woman in the Lynchburg church of whom Cranston was particularly fond]. She hardly holds the place in my affection that she does in yours, but I did appreciate the letter and think it sweet of her to write. While we are on that subject, I might say that if I paid no more attention to your warnings to me than you pay to mine to you, I'd be a dead pigeon. You have simply got to understand that there are a lot of things you can't do and try a little more devotedly to take things easy. I certainly want you to enjoy yourself, but I want to enjoy you also. I won't if you get yourself down and I find you in bed when I return. You say, "I wish I were with you. I'd take care of you." Better, I trust, that you care for yourself. . . .

There is a friendly rat who keeps coming out into the light as I write this to you. He is as black as coal and, unlike most of them in these parts, more the size a rat should be and hence he doesn't jar the earth when he runs. I've had a trap set for some time, but he uses it as a cafeteria. Such are the sights of New Guinea. . . .

Russell

Some days before, Stroup had mailed home a letter to be read on Christmas Day. He felt that he was the chief moral support for each member of his family, as indeed he often was. Through his own loneliness away from home, he inferred the family's longing for him. Thus, he composed with care a message to bind the family together on that day, to express love and encouragement for each person present, and, indeed, to make himself present in the midst of the celebration. The letter portrays the Christmas rituals that I also remember in Lynchburg. Unfortunately, it did not arrive until December 30, though probably we were still all together in Lynchburg to hear it read. Although Stroup despised racism and was a progressive voice in his community, readers will notice that he conveyed his greeting to Hazel, the family's beloved Negro cook, after his greeting to the dog.

"December 25, 1944"

My own family,

Today I shall be criminally AWOL from the army and a deserter from New Guinea, since every moment of the day my heart and mind will be with you all, with nothing left behind but that poor part of me which is slave to the time and distance that would keep us apart. I am sure you will repeat the familiar ritual of Christmas day and so it won't be difficult to follow with you, from the time we awaken to the realization that this is Christmas morning, through the opening of gifts beside the Christmas tree, to the feast that comes at noontime when we have exhausted the possibilities of the gifts, gathered together the wrappings, and left only the chairs piled high with plunder and graced by our Christmas plates of candy, nuts, and all. There will be carols in the house and, I hope, laughter and joy—even though it must be tinged with the sadness we can't very well avoid.

Oddly enough, my greatest joy is this realization: we mean so much to each other that a real Christmas is impossible if we are not together. It is not unusual for families to be bound by ties of love, but I think there is no family that has been as successful as ours in not allowing the passing of the years to weaken in any way that unity of love which remains so real in the sacred circle of our home. There are those who find some lack in Christmas when they cannot be together; for us, indeed, there can be no real Christmas when we are apart.

Our joy must come from remembered Christmases. How many there are of them! How fresh and fine the memories are! I will find myself going back over the years, counting them all. . . . I can recall them in the library at Holyoke; the corner of that lovely living room on the Lake; the apartment on Euclid Avenue; the hurried celebrations before we left for Atwater; that glorious one when Mother came home from the hospital just to make the day complete; in the house next door to the Presbyterian church on Lake Ave.; on Michigan; the rented home in Palo Alto; the memorable ones in the beautiful Webster Street home—Oh, so many, and all so dear!

There is joy in the hope of Christmases to be, next year and many years to come, which I know that God will give to us in answer to our earnest prayers. Could there be a happier day than Christmas 1945 when we shall make amends for the two which we have lost? I can imagine the even better Christmases of eternity when Papa will be with us in more than memory.

We never are apart. Nothing shall be able to separate us from one another; not time nor distance, life or death, nor any other creature. There is a love that can defy them all and we know the secret of it. I am glad right now that our lives were never lived in time alone but also in eternity. Others may find their holiday in gifts and feasts, but for us it has always been "all this and heaven too," for ours has been a holy day which finds its deepest meaning in the love and joy and peace that are eternal. I am grateful for this heritage that makes it possible for me to find Christmas, even here.

You know I shall be with you today, and you will be with me. My first Christmas kiss will be for Mother. As I read over what I have just written I know that you are the one who has made it possible. What Christmas means to me, and shall mean, I owe to you. How can I thank you for all the gifts that you have given? The gift of life itself is the smallest of them, for it would be a little thing without the meaning you have given it for me, and for all of us.

My kiss for Margretta is a tremendous one. You know how much I love you, dear, and always have: from that first day I met you in Mother's arms and knew the wonder of a little sister. They told me

Christmas morning in Lynchburg, Virginia, with, from the left, Emma, an unidentified serviceman invited for Christmas dinner, "General Robert E. Lee," Richard, Margretta, and Cranston. On the mantel are photographs of Margretta and Russell. Hazel is probably behind the camera. Reflected in the mirror are the grand piano and, behind it against the stairway, a large radio that brought news to the attentive family each day.

you were a gift from God, and the years have only confirmed that faith. . . . I have always been proud of you: proud of your beauty, your mind (perhaps the best one of us all), and your heart. I am glad that we can share you now with the world, which through your gifts will have cause to bless you.

What can I find to say to you, Cranston? Since I have been out here I have remembered so much that I felt and never did say. We were too reticent for brothers so close to one another. I started, young, tagging around after you, and I've been tagging ever since. You always found things first, and my part was, and is, "me too." My love for the beautiful and the true found its inspiration in your finding of them. All I attempt to do depends upon your loyal support and your (sometimes foolish) belief in me. Especially during the past ten years I have tried to live up to your expectations. I might possibly do it if only I had the gifts which are yours. I can never mean to the world what you might have meant if your health had permitted, but I promise you I'll do my best. Remember that, more than you will ever know, I depend on you. Together I think we can yet do something—but it must be together.

If Richard were a bit older I'd try to help him understand what he means to us all, and to me. He is "our immortality"—but he could hardly be expected to know what that means. Just tell him for me that no boy ever had an uncle who loved him more. Tell him, too, that I am proud of him, and I know that I will never have cause to be anything else. Dick, old boy, I hope you will have a wonderful, wonderful Christmas even with your Daddy so far away. Take care of your Mother and give her and your Grandma a big hug and kiss for me, and I have an idea they may give it back to you just as I would if I were there.

I hope General lives to share this Christmas with you. This will be the thirteenth, or is it the fourteenth, he has had with us. What an affectionate friend and companion he has been. His heart has always been so much bigger than his little body, and I'm not surprised that it has worn itself out loving us all.

I can't forget Hazel. She, too, has been a member of the family. She has helped to make a lot of Christmases happy for us. A Merry Christmas, Hazel, and a Happy New Year. Thanks a lot for all you have done for the family and for me.

This clumsy letter is overweighted with the load of love it carries. May the Lord keep watch between us while we are absent one from another. Don't forget that I'm on my way home. One of these days my body will catch up with my heart and we will all be together, again.

Russell

Despite this assurance to his family, Stroup was anxious about the impending invasion of the Philippines. He knew it was less than a month away. The 1st Battalion was equipped with ducks, amphibious landing vehicles, and Stroup probably knew that they would go ashore with the first wave. He, and the men with whom he waited, anticipated that the battle to liberate this important outpost of the Japanese empire might be the most difficult they had experienced. He expected to pass his fortieth birthday, January 16, in the midst of that invasion.

Friday, December 22, 1944

Dearest family,

For good and sufficient reason I wish I were one month over forty. I would feel a lot more secure than I do. It is strange how that fatal figure haunts one. I'm sure I shall not mind nearly so much being forty-one. With good luck, I am now midway in my life. Forty years behind me and forty years ahead. . . .

These next ten years will be the years most determinative in the life of the world. It is in these that we shall "grandly gain or meanly lose," as Lincoln said, the last great hope of men. If I am to play a part, it must be in these pregnant years. That goes for all of us. I would like through writing, radio speaking, lecturing, etc., to do my part. I think I can. The church at home, if I serve it, will be my pleasure and my source of income but not my life work in itself. . . .

The best in life, for me, has been you all. . . .

Russell

Emma also had written a special letter for Stroup to open on Christmas Day. That Monday morning Stroup awoke, as he had prophesied, with his heart AWOL but with his head full of the demands of the day. His battalion began loading aboard the ships in the harbor on Christmas afternoon.

Christmas

Dearest family,

I want to write you because it's Christmas morning, and because I love you, and because I haven't written since yesterday, and because "It's Christmas day in the morning." You know I will be thinking of you in spite of everything else I may be doing. And that will be plenty.

The first thing I did this morning was to read your lovely letter, and just sit and dream. It brought you all very close. All that you said about the first Christmas I'll give to my men in the service this morning, so they may share with me the thoughts of one who taught me all I know of Christmas. And I'll read it all over again and again. I'm glad that you will have things as always back home. That's the way I want it and the way I knew you would. In your letter you said that I might be in danger this day, but we can be thankful that this is not so. Lonely we all will be, but I shall be as safe as you, at least for this day. . . .

You remember the song about "three ships come sailing" that we used to sing on Christmas. I can see more than three, and as I look at them I think of our song. Almost everything reminds me of something connected with Christmas at home. There ought to be a law against allowing a sentimentalist like myself to get so far from home.

Yesterday was really our Christmas and, except for the service this morning, which we just had to get in, there can be nothing else, for there are things to do. . . .

Last night was truly fine. Rain threatened but passed by after a few drops. The entertainment was as varied as the [USO] program shows and got the usual generous GI response. It wasn't my choice of a Christmas program, but then I didn't plan it.

I did insist, however, that we should have the carols, and that was quite the most impressive part of the evening. After all the other jazz had quieted down, thirty men took their places on the platform, and before the restless hush of almost two thousand men they sang the old, loved songs of Christmas. When they paused you could hear the sea breaking on the shore as though to remind us of the distance which separated us from home. The stars were bright overhead as they were that night in Bethlehem, and it seemed to me that the angels could not have sung more sweetly than those fine fresh voices. All became very quiet, and out into the darkness rolled the ancient message of joy and peace. It fell as a benediction on all our hearts.

The evening was a long one, but still there were over a hundred men at the candlelight communion service. I wanted us to take this communion together one last time. The platform was softly lighted, but the men sat in darkness. As I called each group forward to kneel in a circle, they would emerge out of the darkness into the light like figures in a Rembrandt, their faces quiet and dignified with the solemnity of the occasion. I think they were coming, truly, into the light of His presence and that the glow of it was in their hearts as well as on their faces. As they went home they were humming the sweet harmony of "Silent Night, Holy Night." It was a good evening. The service this morning will be a good service as I tell them the old, old story. . . .

Darlings, I must close for there is so much to be done. . . .

Russell

Stroup's transport ship, more comfortable than some, set sail the morning after Christmas. His typewriter was stowed, and the next several letters are written in longhand. Without stating that he was on shipboard and headed for battle, Stroup used familiar codes to convey the information.

Wednesday, December 27, 1944

Dearest family,

This is the life I love, however brief, and I shall make the most of it. It will mean a pleasant rest and the enjoyment of comparative luxury. I wish I had all the books I was mailed for Christmas, but so far they have not been received. I shall do what I can with what I have. . . .

You speak of my birthday: I purposely did not send any request for presents because I knew that it would be useless for you to send me any at the time of my birthday. I shall prefer to have them some other time. You will be thinking of me, and that is enough. I hope I will at least receive letters. . . .

All my love to all of you. Don't worry too much about me, for under God I shall be all right wherever I am or whatever I am doing.

Russell

Monday, January 1, 1945

Dearest family,

There is only one way to begin the New Year right, and that's writing to you. As a matter of fact, I didn't quite begin it that way, for I was inveigled into a chess game at a rather late hour last night. My opponent was most distressingly deliberate, which dragged the game out until after midnight. I finally checkmated him in desperation and took myself to my bunk.

We are promised only two meals today: breakfast, which I have had, and a turkey dinner at 2 P.M. I have confirmed this by a glance at the birds themselves in the galley. Since we have no work to do on any day this could hardly be called a "holiday" except for the dinner. But that is something. (Seems as though I'm getting a lot of turkey lately.) So I'll spend the day reading and writing. . . .

All of this is very pleasant in a quiet sort of way. Of course there are some professional duties. I held two services yesterday, one in the morning and one at 6 P.M. The latter was a Communion Service to bring the old year to a proper close and also to meet the requests of those men in the crew who have had no opportunity for some time either to attend a service or to receive communion. They were good services, well attended and appreciated. Naturally, we all need something of the calming influence of worship. It does help.

Concerning 1945, there is only one thought in all our minds—the year may bring us peace and a glad return to home. . . . Even that bright light of hope only pierces the clouds of apprehension that must of necessity hang heavy over the months that lie between this first day of the year and the day of victory and peace. All events must be met with resolution and courage and a faith in the providence of God, which I have in abundance. My message to myself as well as to the men is one King George VI gave on a New Year's Day some years ago [1939]: "I said to the man who stood at the gate of the year, 'Give me a light that I may tread safely into the unknown.' And he replied, 'Go out into the darkness and put your hand into the hand of God. That shall be to you better than light and safer than a known way.' "

Russell

Stroup, following King George, quoted from "Proem" by Minnie Louise Haskens.

Friday, January 5, 1945

Dearest family,

. . . I've been wandering with an old friend in the distant past as I read *Blessed Are the Meek*, a story of Saint Francis. Strange that it should be a "best-seller," and yet not strange, for how tenaciously the human heart holds to the vision implied in such lives. . . . Men would see Jesus, and meet men and women who show that they have learned of him. In all our welter of materialism, sensualism, and confusion, we long for a life of simplicity, purity, and certainty. The persistent question in *Blessed Are the Meek* is "Can men actually live the life of our Lord?" Francis thought one could. Most of us only hope it may be possible. Or, rather, one part of us hopes it might be, while the rest of us is too earthbound to venture to leave all and follow him. Unfortunately we follow our lower yearnings, but there is hope for us in the vision that will not die, however disobedient we may be toward it.

My whole life has been haunted by that vision, never realized. We have approached it but never found it. Couldn't we try, if the chance is given to us, to achieve a greater simplicity of life, more free from the burden of "things" and more truly dedicated to God? Yet I know how I love "things" and how loath I am to leave all and follow Him! In the army I have done so in a measure. Here is imposed upon us poverty, chastity, and obedience. But the satisfaction one might gain from that is spoiled by the purpose which brings us together, and by the separation from friends and family. I don't think that the absolute poverty, chastity, or obedience of Francis are good, but I do think the emphasis on simplicity, purity, and dedication is what all the world needs. . . .

I have also been wandering along the Mississippi with Huckleberry Finn as I reread that wonderful tale. It made me think a lot of Cranston, remembering how he loves it, and how we read it together. Not a bad way to spend the time.

We play chess. I know how, better than most, but I'm careless. If I used my head I'd win, but I don't sometimes. I lose when there is no necessity for it, or else I get behind and then have to work like fury to save myself. That is the part I like: to pull victory out of certain defeat. I'm funny: I don't like to lose—makes me mad at myself—but neither do I like to win—that embarrasses me terribly and I feel the necessity to apologize. I was never meant to play games. . . .

I thought I'd do some writing, but that hasn't been possible—too many people in too close spaces. Also, too much on my mind, I guess. Can't help thinking. Tomorrow, and tomorrow, and tomorrow.

But the immediate tomorrow is Sunday with services to be held. I think I'll preach again from Joshua, "Be strong, be of good courage, be not afraid, neither be thou dismayed, for lo, the Lord thy God is with thee whithersoever thou goest." It's a good text. It demands something of us and expects something of God. I like the picture of a man in the might of his own manhood, sustained as he must be by the unfailing power of God—an undefeatable combination. I have great compassion for weakness, but I don't like it.

I've thought how wonderful it would be if, in times of peace, a great country like ours could send convoys of young people on peaceful voyages to other lands—great invasions of goodwill, tourists with a purpose—to learn of other people and to be known by them. Why couldn't that be possible? I could write a book on all the things we do in war which might be duplicated in peace for a creative purpose, if only we had the will to do it, or the good sense.

The Philippine Islands. From Smith, Triumph in the Philippines *(1963; rpt. Washington, D.C.: Center of Military History, U.S. Army, 1993), 20.*

Here we have a government intimately concerned with the health of ten million fighting men, that they may be strong and efficient killers. Why not be concerned with the health of ten million workers, creators not destroyers? . . .

Let's all take good care of ourselves and put our trust in God, who will surely give us the joy of a glad reunion. I reckon the sufferings of this present time are not worthy to be compared to the joy of that day. Love,

Russell

The assault convoy carrying 175,000 troops, surrounded by the largest American fleet yet assembled in the Pacific, stretched more than forty miles as it sailed two thousand miles from New Guinea northwest to Luzon, the northern and principal island of the Philippine Archipelago. The convoy steamed past Manila and north toward Lingayen Gulf. The plan was for the invasion force to advance southward down the broad valley toward Manila. On the morning of January 8, one day before the scheduled landing, the convoy came under heavy, sustained attack from Japanese kamikaze pilots, directed particularly at the escort carriers. One carrier was too severely damaged to continue. That evening Stroup prayed, and wrote.

Monday, January 8, 1945

Dearest family,

. . . Tonight will be my Passover experience before Good Friday. I know the Lord will be with me then and I shall receive in Spirit the broken bread and the cup as a surety that this is true and all is well. The Via Dolorosa is not pleasant. If in some minor way I can be a Simon, to ease the burden of the cross that will rest heavy on the shoulders of these men, then I may feel that inasmuch as I have done it unto the least of these mine will be the blessed privilege of carrying the Cross of Christ. That sounds pretty pretentious and I didn't mean it that way, but I feel it most sincerely, and it is my good comfort.

I have been singing in my mind, "So long Thy power hath led me, sure it still will lead me on, o'er moor and fen, o'er crag and torrent, till the night is gone," only I change the next verse to read, "And with the morn of peace, your faces smile, all I have loved long since, and lost awhile." The "awhile" has been a tragedy for us all, but confidently I anticipate the morning and home and you. Love to you all,

Russell

In his letters, Stroup rarely crossed out a phrase to select one more apt. In this letter he first wrote, "If in some minor way I can be a Simon to bear the cross that will rest heavily on the shoulders of these men." He then crossed out "to bear the cross" and replaced it with "to ease the burden of the cross." The cross was theirs. His role was to ease the weight.

8

"A Thrilling Experience Long to Be Remembered"

Dearest family,

As MacArthur says, "We have returned." It has been a thrilling experience long to be remembered. Four days have passed, each one with its share of noteworthy news. I wish I could tell you all of it.

You will have heard that by the grace of God and the confusion of the Japanese we have so far been fortunate in escaping the more disagreeable features of an invasion. When I came ashore with the assault troops from a gulf swarming with a giant armada, my heart was in my mouth and there was that queer empty feeling in my stomach, but it was all premature. It was fearfully hot riding in an LVT [landing vehicle, tracked]—I was with the spearhead of the assault—but we did make time. I had said a word of prayer with each assault force as they put out from the mother ship, to prepare them for what we had every reason to expect, and I had tried to prepare myself. Our prayers were answered more surely than we had hoped. The trial by fire did not come, and my first days ashore have been quite different from the remembered days of tragedy in New Guinean assaults.

We pushed cautiously if rapidly inland and came to our first native barrio (small settlement) where Filipinos came out of their dugouts to welcome us. Some had been wounded by our bombardment, all had been suffering from terror during those hours when the great guns pounded their shore. Yet their welcome was wonderful. This was our first contact with a reception that has been continuous and heartwarming.

One ragged, smiling individual offered me an egg, and we fell into conversation. "You are so welcome! We are so happy you are here!

All that we have is yours!" These were not idle words. We have been overwhelmed by kindness.

As we proceeded over rice fields and beside fish ponds we came constantly upon settlements. From the most sparsely settled country in the world we have arrived at one of the most thickly populated. Everywhere, the people stood in smiling groups, waving their hands, shouting their greetings. The favorite expressions are "Victory!" "Good Luck!" "Welcome!" "We are so glad you are come!" "Thank you! Thank you!"

There were a few scattered pockets of resistance, easily overcome, but mostly it has been a triumphant procession. We have seen houses again, most of them huts yet very attractive on their high stilts. There are cultivated fields, sugarcane, rice, corn, bananas, coconuts. I saw one GI with his arms around a little native pony. "Gosh," he said, "It's good to see a horse again." There are some horses hitched to gaily painted carts, but mostly the means of locomotion are Brahman bullocks and water buffalo—great horned creatures with some tiny tyke astride them.

We spent our first night back on the LVT, which meant little if any sleep, huddled together as we were, and on the alert for the enemy.

With the 1st Battalion, 1st Regiment, 6th Infantry Division, 6th Army, Stroup landed on "Blue 1" Beach. This battalion, equipped with amphibious LVTs, advanced to its left along coastal roads toward the Bued River. After spending the night in these vehicles, the men proceeded upriver the next morning to the town of Mangaldan, where they discovered that other battalions from their division were already in place.

In the early morning of the second day we arrived at our first town of any size and saw a railroad, electric wires, small but substantial buildings and—wonder of wonder, after months in New Guinea—paved streets. There was an ornate public square with a rococo bandstand in the center, flanked on each side with gaudy statues of Filipino heroes. Troops were dug in all over the square, busy cooking breakfast. I was able to wash and shave and boil my precious egg along with two others presented to me by the townspeople.

Then I began to look around. Crowds of natives, most of whom understand English and many of whom speak it fluently, gathered around me, firing questions about the news of the world from which

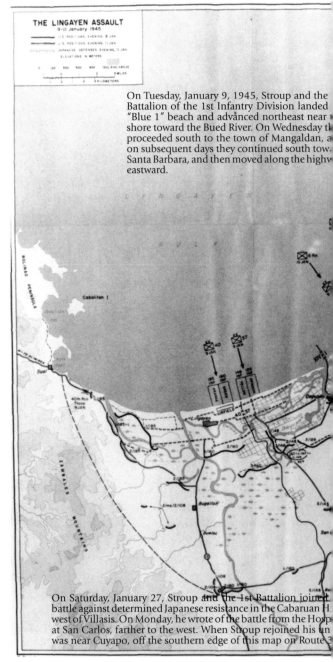

THE LINGAYEN ASSAULT
9-11 January 1945

On Tuesday, January 9, 1945, Stroup and the
Battalion of the 1st Infantry Division landed
"Blue 1" beach and advanced northeast near
shore toward the Bued River. On Wednesday th
proceeded south to the town of Mangaldan, a
on subsequent days they continued south tow.
Santa Barbara, and then moved along the highw
eastward.

On Saturday, January 27, Stroup and the 1st Battalion joined
battle against determined Japanese resistance in the Cabaruan H
west of Villasis. On Monday, he wrote of the battle from the Hosp
at San Carlos, farther to the west. When Stroup rejoined his un
was near Cuyapo, off the southern edge of this map on Route

The Lingayan assault. From Smith, Triumph in the
Philippines, *map I.*

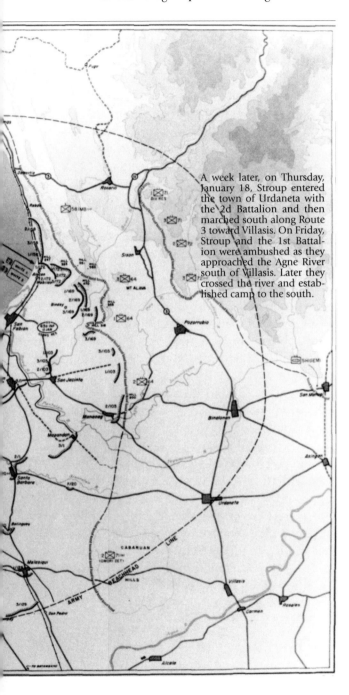

A week later, on Thursday, January 18, Stroup entered the town of Urdaneta with the 2d Battalion and then marched south along Route 3 toward Villasis. On Friday, Stroup and the 1st Battalion were ambushed as they approached the Agne River south of Villasis. Later they crossed the river and established camp to the south.

they have been so long separated. Their comments were intelligent and their interest touching. . . .

We marched across country toward our objective, a little inland town. But we were never out of touch with people. We went through a field where a farmer in a ragged pair of shorts stood by the side of the path, in his hand a large palm leaf platter piled high with roasted peanuts. As our straggling line of GIs went past, each soldier responded to the peasant's smiling invitation and dipped out a great handful of the fragrant nuts and then munched them as we went along. The kindly courtesy of that Filipino is characteristic of our welcome.

We took a break near a farmhouse. We were met by a courtly schoolteacher, his doctor brother, and some of the prettiest and best-dressed girls we have seen—which greatly cheered the hearts of the soldiers. Our impromptu hosts had cut coconuts in two, then filled glasses with the cool, tasty coconut milk and shredded the soft meat in the shell. Each coconut half had a spoon in it. They handed these, together with a glass of coconut milk, to the hot and tired soldiers. The girls, having heard I was a chaplain, flocked around me—much to the envy of less fortunate GIs. I fear the girls mistook me for a priest, as one told of her ambition to become a nun. I did not disillusion them but basked in their attention.

At a crossroads by a school, I found the yard of a more preten- tious house filled with soldiers. The resident was a former official. Anticipating the arrival of the U.S. troops he had prepared great plat- ters of chicken, which were passed around by his servants, attractive daughters, and charming wife. They also served coffee, a very scarce commodity, sweetened with rum. The chicken, assaulted by hundreds of soldiers, soon ran out and yet the coffee seemed as inexhaustible as the graciousness of our host. One very lovely daughter pumped water from the well by the hour to fill the canteens of the soldiers, who were more refreshed by her smiling beauty than by the cool water itself.

As you can tell, all this is far different from war as we have known it in New Guinea, or I think anywhere, for even the men with us who served in France say it was never like this.

Much love to all,

Russell

The Japanese were not "confused," as Stroup suggested in the letter above. The U.S. armada had entered Lingayen Gulf at the northwest end of Luzon's central plain. Manila was situated on a bay at the southern end of this plain, a hundred miles distant. Rather than contest the landing, the Japanese had positioned 250,000 well-equipped troops in defensive positions in the mountains to the east and to the west of the broad plain, and in the Cabaruan Hills outcropping in the center of the plain, in the hope that they might eventually encircle and decimate the American army as it moved south toward Manila. This strategy was reminiscent of Biak, but here the Japanese force was vastly larger. The battle for the island of Luzon would become one of the most difficult of the war.

Stroup's division was in the center of the invasion forces and as it moved south toward Santa Barbara encountered only light resistance during the first few days.

Stroup's first letter following the landing was handwritten. Later that same day his typewriter was delivered to him, and he immediately resumed correspondence. It is apparent that the 6th Division appreciated Stroup's exceptional gifts, expected a great deal from him, and gave him strong support. Tom Williamsen, the sharpshooter deputized to Stroup as chaplain's assistant, was a critical part of that support. It was Williamsen's duty to provide Stroup with some protection. This he did with growing determination, despite Stroup's tendency to slip away in order to spare Williamsen the dangers to which Stroup was willing to expose himself.

Saturday, January 13, 1945

Dearest family,

This is, so far as I know, the only typewriter this far forward in the U.S. Army. . . . My former letter brought you up to January eleventh. I'll take up from there.

We reached a strategic crossroads on Wednesday night, which we secured after a brush with the Japanese. They had hardly retreated, leaving behind their dead and a burning truck, before the Filipinos were dousing the fire on the truck and dismantling it, carrying off those prized pieces that they were able to secure. We dug in for the night. I spent a rather cold and wakeful ten hours in my foxhole. In the morning we faced the problem of food: the rapidity of our movement has outstripped our supplies, and the combat rations that we had carried with us were exhausted.

The saint who cares for the hungry sent me a ministering angel in the form of a Filipino who provided us with two eggs. This, plus a papaya melon, made a delicious breakfast—save for the absence of coffee, which for me is a catastrophe. Our camp was soon besieged by friendly Filipinos eager to serve us. They filled canteens, brought water in helmets for bathing, built fires, and cooked food for us. I contracted with a sweet-faced old lady to bring me a roast chicken in exchange for a bar of soap, a very scarce commodity, and she brought it at noontime. It had been barbecued over a charcoal fire and was quite a feast, though the local birds are rather lean and tough. For her labor of love, we added a chocolate bar for her to take to her children. . . .

The natives love to work for us, but especially to talk to us. They are great talkers. Some come wounded or sick and we treat them at the aid station, for which they are most grateful. In consequence, the doctors and the aid men get the major share of the eggs and chickens. Already we have faced the difficulties natural to the presence of many civilians where fighting is going on, and this will become more acute as we meet greater resistance from the Japanese. I fear that many will suffer the tragedy of a people caught in the conflict. But they seem to harbor not the slightest resentment that they might become victims of the war, so happy are they in their deliverance. . . .

Our men are having a truly wonderful time. As never before, they realize what we are fighting for as it is expressed in human terms. This was so unreal in New Guinea, but here the joy of the people over their deliverance is ample compensation for whatever suffering we may have to undergo. Here are men and women who have known both liberty and slavery and can appreciate the difference. As one soldier said, "The people back home will never appreciate us like the natives do out here." The Filipino is flamboyantly patriotic, which is an antidote to the patriotic lethargy of the average American.

Those of us who have at times regretted the necessity of service gain fresh enthusiasm from ragged peons clamoring to enlist in the army. I talked with one who came in from the hills, proudly displaying an old type army .45 revolver which he had saved from his seven enlistments in the U.S. Army, where he had served for over twenty years. He was captured at Bataan but later, like most of the Filipinos, released from prison camp. His clothes were in tatters, but he had a campaign hat, a very snappy salute, and an eager desire for an M-1 rifle and a chance at the Japanese.

Into our headquarters this morning came an old gray-haired man with his honorable discharge from the U.S. Army received in 1930 after thirty years of service. Erect as a ramrod he came to attention, saluted proudly, and said, "I want to enlist." . . .

Last night two neighboring farmers dug a foxhole for me and Tom, brought hay to fill it, water for us to wash in, and some "camotes" and barbecued chicken. The "camote" is a root, much like a sweet potato, only better. It was served to us on a platter in the center of which was a bowl filled with hot brown sugar syrup, into which you dipped the boiled camotes. I found them delicious. I would not have you think that all the soldiers are faring as sumptuously as we are, but somehow we have been lucky. . . .

There is little to tell of military activities even if I were permitted to do so. . . . So far, for our particular regiment, it has been pretty easy going. We have the stuff, and in this open terrain we have a chance to use it. The skies are swept clean by our planes. We can hardly expect to continue our initial success, but we are on the march. The signposts on the road point the way and we are marching forward along a victory highway lined with a liberated people cheering us on.

Much love to you all,

Russell

Among the division's chaplains, Stroup was senior in experience. He kept a close eye on units in danger, and also on some chaplains who were willing to appear at the front only after fighting had subsided.

Monday, January 15, 1945

Dearest family,

Tomorrow I will celebrate two anniversaries; the seventh day of the campaign and the fortieth year of my somewhat varied earthly pilgrimage. There was a time a few weeks ago when I began to wonder whether I would reach that age when life is supposed to begin, but with only one more day to go I'm a bit more optimistic, particularly as things have been going fairly well.

Saturday and Sunday did show something of a change in pace, with a bit more of the sort of thing one might expect. I had word that one of our battalions was having it a bit rough and thought I'd better go forward since only the Catholic chaplain was with them. When I arrived I found that he was not there as I had supposed, and he had promised. The men, without any chaplain, had casualties to care for, so I stayed on with them, ministering to the wounded and the dying and dead. We were under fire by artillery and small arms, and while it was not as bad as I have seen it was bad enough to give me plenty to do.

The small notebook that Stroup carried in his pocket during the Philippine campaign has been preserved. On this day he recorded: "9 dead, 7 Protestants to bury, one C.O. leading his company, one aid man rescuing wounded. Aid men get too little credit for very dangerous work." In the back of his notebook he recorded the names of the dead along with their serial numbers, religious affiliations, addresses where possible, and such circumstances of death as he could determine. "Salari, Daniel . . . Jan. 13, Sharpshooter, head." "Thomas, Norman P. . . . Prot., Jan. 13, sniper, night attack, rifle, chest wound." "Phillips, Gerald W. . . . Prot., Medical Detail, shot through forehead bringing in wounded, January 14."

It was impossible to have services for the men on Sunday, but I did manage to have prayer with each group going out on patrol or to the lines, and that was helpful. I stayed with the unit until late Sunday afternoon, by which time the action had died down, the objective had been reached, and the Catholic chaplain came forward to relieve me. I then returned to my regular battalion, which is still in reserve, and I'm with them now.

It is strange to be fighting in a country where there are so many people; to have crowds around the positions which are under fire; men, women and children, most of them pouring into our lines for greater protection, but still facing considerable peril to themselves and often becoming a problem to us. You look over open fields toward the enemy position and it all seems so peaceful, with cattle grazing on the sides of the hill and peaceful little farmhouses so quiet in the sun. But men are fighting and dying out there. It seems even more incongruous to advance, as we did, down a broad cement highway with mileage signs and warnings to "Go Slow, School Children." . . .

No mail yet, of course. Hope some will come for my birthday, but doubt it.

Russell

Stroup's notebook for that day recounts a military problem not often reported: "Jan. 15th, Monday—Bad eggs & pork for breakfast laid up 72 men from Headquarters. Men lying everywhere, vomiting, etc. Others, including myself, not quite so sick. I only ate a couple mouths full but suffered from diarrhea and felt punk all afternoon. . . . Moved late in afternoon to new

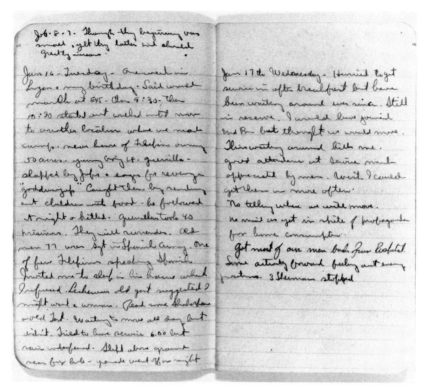

Stroup's Philippine notebook, open to the entry for his fortieth birthday.

location. I rode truck, too weak to walk. Spent night and felt better next day. Dug in in field heavily fertilized, I think, by human excrement, and suffered from stench. Rained, which added nothing to comfort in foxhole. Heard a lot of activity in the night."

The next day, Stroup's fortieth birthday, continued a pattern of inactivity that he found frustrating. "Jan. 16—Tuesday—One week in Luzon & my birthday. Said would march at 8:45—then 9:30—then 10:30 started out walked until noon to another location where we made camp, near house of Filipino owning 50 acres. . . . Old man was Sgt. in Spanish Army. One of few Filipinos speaking Spanish. Invited me to sleep in his house, which I refused. Lecherous old gent suggested I might want a woman. Read some Shakespeare and Old Test." Which Shakespeare passages Stroup selected for his birthday meditations we do not know, but in the Old Testament his mood led him to the Book of Job. There he found, in the mouth of one of

Job's "comforters," a motto that he appropriated for himself. He wrote in the margin at the top of the page, above his entry for the day: "Job 8.1. 'Though thy beginning was small, yet thy latter end should greatly increase.'"

His day remained one of frustration, into the evening and through the night. "Waiting to move all day but didn't. Tried to have service 6:00 but rain interfered. Slept aboveground near foxhole—grenade went off in night."

Stroup awoke to continued, galling inactivity. "January 17th, Wednesday —Hurried to get service in after breakfast but have been waiting around ever since. Still in reserve. I would have joined 2d Bat but thought we would move. This waiting around kills me. Good attendance at Service, much appreciated by men. Wish I could work them in more often. No telling when we will move. No mail as yet."

Later that day, however, Stroup did break free and go forward to join the 2d Battalion. On Thursday morning the men entered the burning town of Urdaneta. They then marched south along Route 3, the principal highway in the valley, toward Villasis and the Agno River beyond. On Friday his own amphibious unit moved up to assist with the river crossing. There would be no more time for reflective entries in the notebook. Stroup began his next letter home on Sunday evening.

Sunday, January 21, 1945

Dearest family,

. . . A great deal has been happening recently. I'll do my best to tell you about it, although writing is a bit difficult with the crowd of Filipino children who are all about my typewriter admiring very vocally my dexterity, which would be greater if they were not distracting me as they most certainly do. I haven't the heart to drive them away. I am not certain whether we have taken over the Philippines or they have taken over us.

Just after I had written to you last, I received word that the 2d Battalion was to make a forward movement and so I went to join them. I found the headquarters rather grimly set up in a cemetery with foxholes among the graves. This didn't seem particularly propitious for the beginning of any engagement, but I lay there in the safety of a foxhole while the artillery and mortars laid down a tremendous barrage on the town where the Japanese were holding out with a comparatively small force and some tanks. When the barrage lifted, there was the stunning moment of silence which follows an intense period of noise, and we moved forward. I went with one of the assault companies. We moved cautiously to the town, which by now was a flaming inferno, the lightly constructed houses burning like tinder. It seemed hardly possible that anyone could remain there alive, and so it must have been, for we heard no shots and saw no enemy. It was hot as Hades and we were thankful indeed to pass beyond the limits of the town to the shade of trees and the coolness of fields bounded by irrigation ditches, even though here the enemy was more likely to be found. As it happened, the elements on our left were meeting all of the opposition. While we made our way cautiously, it was a progress without incident: just a little opposition, and most of the Japanese retired rapidly.

By afternoon we had consolidated our gains and were awaiting further orders, which were some time in coming. Our colonel asked for permission to move off on his own, which was given him, and we made our way down a cement highway toward a town that was to be the objective for the next advance. Along this way we found nothing, but as we advanced we saw groups coming from all directions across the rice fields; little knots of people by twos and threes, dozens, and then scores. They had caught sight of our troops and were emerging from their hiding places to welcome us.

The miles we marched were lined with welcoming civilians. One old man, wrinkled and wizened, without a tooth in his white-thatched head, danced up and down wildly like a little boy, shouting greetings to us in Spanish (only a few old people still speak it) at the top of his aged voice. Tears streamed down his furrowed cheeks as I gave him my hand, which he pressed to his lips. A little further on, in a crowd of citizens, there was one man wearing a khaki shirt on which was pinned a cross, a Boy Scout badge, and two Salvation Army buttons. I found in questioning him that he belonged to the Salvation Army and had served for a while as an unofficial chaplain in the Filipino forces. . . .

The next day we pressed onward by forced march to the river, which was our objective, meeting no opposition on the way. There we stopped in a fairly large town. It was quite deserted when we arrived, but not for long, as almost at once the civilians returned. . . .

The 2d Battalion settled down to guard its positions, but meanwhile the men of the 1st had moved forward. I planned to join them when they pushed through us and beyond. They came down the road in the armored troop carriers called LVTs, used for crossing water, as the river lay ahead. I picked a ride on the third in the column, which turned out to be something of a mistake.

We had proceeded only a short way toward our crossing when the enemy, dug in and concealed, opened fire. The fire spattered over our LVT, some hitting just above my head and—although I didn't know it at the moment—wounding an Indian boy who stood beside me, Chief Charlie, a good friend of mine. He didn't know he was wounded either, for a few minutes. Meanwhile the call had come for someone to get out and walk back for litter bearers. There was a certain reluctance to get out of the shelter of the vehicles, exposed as one would be to enemy fire, but since the rest of them were needed there, I decided to go. I climbed out and started down the column until I came to the one carrying the battalion aid station. There I secured a litter squad and started back to the front.

Before we reached the wounded man, who was way forward, we were pinned down by a murderous fire that kept us under cover for a number of minutes. When it let up a bit, we crawled forward to the wounded man, got him on the litter, and started our slow journey back. We had lost one of the four litter bearers somewhere in the shuffle. I think he felt safer staying in the ditch, and so I carried one end of the litter. It was hard going, for our patient was heavy. Every now and then we had to put him down and take cover, and constantly the bullets were whining over our heads. I hadn't noticed who it was when I put him on the litter, but at our first stop I tried to speak to him and found it was a boy who had played music in our services—a very nice fellow. I don't think he was wounded fatally; he certainly accepted his rough carry without complaint.

We got to the aid station, which had been set up meanwhile, and then started back for more wounded—or rather another litter squad started back and I with them. This trip was a duplicate of the other, starting and stopping, but finally reaching our objective. We found a wounded lad, and while two of the aid men were caring for him I found refuge in a ditch. One of the aid men was adjusting a bandage when a sniper bullet hit him. I went at once to his side but he was either unconscious or dead. I managed to find the driver of a jeep stopped nearby, and we got the wounded man and the body on it and went back.

The lad was dead when we reached the station. Too much credit cannot be given to the aid men. The percentage of casualties among them is high, and their work is difficult and dangerous. Having had a tiny bit of experience carrying men out under fire I know what it must be for them, for whom this is expected routinely.

Altogether during this skirmish I made four trips forward and back with wounded men. It was an exciting time, the more so since it was quite unexpected. That vicinity had been cleared of the enemy, or so we thought, but they had moved back during the night. There was only a handful, but a handful of determined men, well dug in, who expect to die, can do a lot of damage to a vastly superior force. Our casualties were what the reports would call "light," although I hate to use that phrase since one casualty is a tragedy too grievous for words.

Once we had cleaned out this pocket of resistance, our progress was unimpaired. We crossed the river and then set out on foot along our way. We passed gingerly by a number of spots where the enemy might have set up a very advantageous defense, but there was none. The Japanese pass by the obvious and spring the unexpected. . . .

Our last stop, which has lasted over a day now, was near a little town—quite deserted when we reached it but filled with people now. Here we had our Sunday services—the first time since we landed that I have had the opportunity.

My first service was with C Company at nine o'clock. I walked there, for it was not far away. My congregation was entirely GI, and a very good one. I talked to them of the experiences of the past few days, how truly fortunate we had been, and how important it was that we should offer thanks to God for His providential care. The general had said our success was due to Preparation and Luck. I reminded the men that, for us, "luck" was a poor description of God. I also used as a text the words of our Lord when he said that he had come to heal the brokenhearted, deliver the captive, etc. We were surely conscious in these days that we had been instruments in the hands of God to accomplish this glorious ministry. We had seen a brokenhearted people leap for joy and a captive people emerge from bondage.

My next service was near headquarters, and there we had a lot of Philippine citizens in attendance, most of them Protestants who had not had a real service for three years since their pastors, being mainly Americans, had been interred. I gave them New Testaments, which were much appreciated. The Filipinos insisted on donating a collection that consisted of four hen eggs, one duck egg, a platter of camotes, a bunch of bananas, and the promise of a laundry job on my soiled fatigues. Such a collection might complicate the work of the deacons at First Church Lynchburg, but out here I knew just how to dispose of it with a minimum of bookkeeping. Since I used the same subject for this service, the natives were much moved, and loud in their gratitude.

I then got a jeep and, with our machine gun manned and my assistant with rifle at the ready, we started to the forward element of our command. All morning they had been shelling with mortars a detachment of Japanese who, supported by several tanks, might have decided to attack. However we had our service uninterrupted, save by the noise of the mortar fire, which fortunately was not returned by the Japanese while we were there.

We made the trip back without incident and then started out at once, without lunch, for the 2d Battalion, still without a chaplain. There I held a service at about two o'clock. It was not as much of a success, for just before I got there they had received a very unexpected attack by a small force of Japanese. A good deal of excitement prevailed, and most of the men were forced to stay at their positions. I had picked up the Catholic chaplain at regimental headquarters and he had his Mass while I had our service. We then returned to our respective homes.

I managed to get some food and started to write this letter, but the interruptions were many and finally became so great that I had to quit altogether, and take it up again this morning. Yesterday our camp looked like a county fair with all the families out, walking from position to position talking with the men—who themselves were busy passing out candy and cigarettes and receiving gifts in return. The men were also doing a lot of photography, of the girls especially. I myself got a couple of such pictures in the morning. As I was driving out to the forward position for service, we passed through a little barrio where there were a number of girls on each side of the narrow road, loaded with flowers which they began to throw at our jeep. I stopped to take their picture, much to their delight, and we then accepted the flowers, which filled our vehicle with a fragrant offering. On the way back I found a detachment of Filipino recruits drawn up under two American flags, ready to join up with our army. The flags, appearing bright and new, must have been secreted during the occupation.

The Filipinos are interested in everything and insist on examining everything. It may interest Margretta to know that my pictures of her were much admired. One beauty parlor operator made many notes on her coiffure, dress, and so forth, for future use—so if the local gals appear with hairdos *à la Austin*, that is the reason. They were also thrilled by the pictures of our home and furniture—and like everyone else, Mother, skeptical that anyone so young could be the mother of an old man like myself.

I talked with the local priest and asked whether he had met any Christian Japanese. He said that one Japanese Catholic, a private, had come to him for confession and communion. He spoke no English or Filipino, but made his confession in Japanese and received his absolution in Latin. As the priest said, "We did not understand each other, but the good God knew." . . .

I have a lot of work to do getting out letters of condolence—not so many, thank God, as on previous campaigns. . . .

I am feeling better physically than I have since leaving home. My jungle rot is clearing up and, except for some aches and pains from marching, and sleeping on the ground, I am in great shape. Since blackout is in force, we get lots of sleep, and now that our kitchens have caught up with us, plenty to eat. I pray God we may continue to be as fortunate as we have been so far. Meanwhile I send you all my dearest love.

Russell

Throughout the Japanese occupation, some Filipinos and a few Americans hid in the hills to fight on as guerrillas. In a letter addressed to Cranston alone, Stroup shared some stories that their mother would not appreciate (though of course she would read them). Whatever Stroup's feeling about the cruelties that war and occupation engender, it must have been helpful to be able to share the reality that he encountered.

Tuesday, January 23, 1945

Dearest Cranston,

. . . This is a very interesting country and our days are replete with fascinating experiences quite different from New Guinea. I think you would get a particular kick out of the guerrillas, who are quite picturesque, as the name implies, have done a wonderful job, and are cooperating in a superb manner with our troops.

This morning we were sending out a patrol to root out a cave of Japanese, and this guerrilla was standing by so I asked him—he is a good friend, and a Protestant—whether he was going along. He answered, "I hope so but I don't know whether they'll let me." When he found that they would, he was quite satisfied.

There was one young lad, not a regular guerrilla, but with aspirations, fifteen years old and eager to revenge himself for a slap administered by a Jap soldier. He worked with his little sister, aged ten, in a twosome of extermination. The little girl would go out into the fields where the Japanese soldiers might be hiding, with a basket of eggs. Hungry, a soldier would spy her and ask for, or demand, eggs. She, of course, gave them out, remembered the spot, and told her brother. In the night he would creep out, bolo knife in hand, and there would be one less of the enemy in the morning. It is a cruel story but shows the fighting spirit of this people, which exists irrespective of age.

The Americans with the guerrillas are a romantic lot, to judge by the stories that come to us. I was talking with a guerrilla this morning who told me of one American, a former mining engineer, who joined up and was placed in command of an active unit that did much damage to the Japanese. They sent a large force to apprehend him, but without avail until they took his wife and child as hostages, and threatened them, whereupon he voluntarily gave himself up and is presumed to be dead.

Many of the guerrillas are armed only with knives; some have revolvers of ancient lineage, old army .45s, .38s, and even .32s. They look like the desperadoes of the old West and are quite as free and easy on the draw. Many had Japanese rifles, but they are discarding these, for the danger is too great of Americans mistaking them for the enemy if they are seen with enemy rifles.

We are, for the first time, static for a couple of days and are set up in a schoolhouse. I am writing on the principal's desk, a nice mahogany job with a chair to match. I'm living with some other officers in the Home Economics building, three small rooms that had been at one time a model home for teaching the natives how to live. There was a bedstead in it without slats, springs, or mattress. I appropriated it, put boards across, laid my air mattress on it, and slept last night for the first time in a real bed. At least it was under cover and above the dust of the floor, where the other officers slept—they having been behind me in appropriating. . . .

Be good and take care of yourself and Mother. Your loving brother,

Russell

9

"I Think I Did My Part"

In his letter of May 24, 1944, Stroup had been anxious about the morale of the American soldier and wondered whether his own support for the pacifist criticisms of big-power conflicts following the First World War might have contributed to a culture of cynicism. A month later he would learn at Biak just how brave and determined the American soldier could be. He would come to interpret the soldiers' apparent cynicism as free men's hatred of warfare— a paradoxical virtue on the battlefield and a hopeful sign for democratic reconstruction following the war.

During the summer of 1944, Stroup had been anxious to return to "a nice soft job" in Washington. By the time of the Philippine landing, however, he had recovered his physical stamina and deepened his spiritual dedication. Although his letters anticipated a return home during that year, his spirit was fully focused on the immediate task. The day before the landing, Stroup achieved a transfiguring insight. Many of the fine young soldiers with whom he served, innocent of the evils that had precipitated this great war, might die in the days ahead. They were bearing the burden of the sins of the age. They were modern Christs, whose blood might be required to redeem the age. "If in some minor way I can be a Simon, to ease the burden of the cross that will rest heavy on the shoulders of these men, . . . mine will be the blessed privilege of carrying the Cross of Christ."

That insight answered Struop's morbid dread that he might not reach his fortieth birthday. Once he accepted that calling, he ceased to worry about tempering his behavior. Gone were the assurances home that "I will take good care of myself." Instead, he was everywhere, determined to uphold those troops who were in the greatest danger.

Rumors may have circulated in the amphibious unit to which Stroup was assigned that when the coastal and river areas around Lingayen Gulf were secured, the unit would be withdrawn for rest, then dispatched to land at Hong Kong, the nearest point on the China mainland. (The navy favored landings on the China coast, but MacArthur opposed them, and they never took place.) On a page near the back of his notebook, Stroup imagined the following schedule for the conclusion of his military tour:

January, February, in combat, Philippines
March, April, May, in rest, Philippines
June, July, August, in combat, China
September, home

Below that he drew pictures of Pacific theater ribbons: the New Guinea ribbon with three combat stars affixed; the Philippines ribbon with one; China, with one. Then he listed his combat engagements.

Hollandia, Biak, Sansapor,
Lingayen, Hong Kong

Finally he projected his total military experience: "36 months in army, 20 months overseas, 11 months in combat." Clearly Stroup wanted to remain with the troops and to finish his military tour by visiting the one great Pacific theater he had not seen, China.

In his first letter from Biak, June 1, 1944, Stroup had written, "I have been in wonderful ways protected by a Providence who must be moved by your prayers in my behalf. For that I am grateful, although I have a guilty feeling of special privilege not accorded to so many men who have suffered or died." Now he had resolved this guilt. With both personal pride and total trust that Providence would continue to protect him no matter what, he set all cautions aside and resolved to be present with every wounded or dying man he could reach.

I find Stroup's posture to be magnificent but also foolhardy and, in the end, untenable. He seemed to demand special divine protection day after day. He tells of one act of protection in the final letter that has been preserved; a second guardian would appear a few days thereafter.

Several divisions were advancing rapidly southward, despite the large Japanese force that remained entrenched in the Cabaruan Hills that rose in the middle of the valley. Army units sent into the hills on January seventeenth to eliminate Japanese resistance thought they had accomplished that task after several days' fighting in which they killed five hundred of the enemy. After most of the army troops had withdrawn to continue their southward march, the garrison that remained was attacked on January 20 and 21 by

a previously undiscovered Japanese force and suffered heavy casualties. In
response, a 1st Infantry battalion was dispatched to the hills on January 24,
but it soon found itself pinned down as well. On Saturday, January 27, the
1st Battalion, with which Stroup served, was dispatched.

Monday, January 29, 1945

Dearest family,

I have only time for a very brief letter which cannot in any sense
review the events of the past three days. They have been very difficult
ones in which our organization was called upon to take some strongly
fortified positions in the hills. Considering the task given us, I think
we may be thankful that our losses were as small as they were, but still
the heart aches for the boys wounded and dead, and for their families.
Fortunately, now it is over for the time being. . . .

I think I did my part from the time the first attack was made until
the end. Before the men took off, in the lull between the barrage
and the zero hour, I went from foxhole to foxhole having a prayer
with the men there and pretty well covered one of the two companies taking part. Whether by chance or otherwise, that company was
remarkably fortunate and suffered fewer casualties than any other.
Several of the wounded men later told me of the comfort that prayer
had been, and how they felt that God had truly protected them in their
ordeal.

I followed along with this company until the wounded began going
back, at which time I returned to the aid station, where I worked with
the wounded men as they were brought in from all units. As there were
lulls, I went forward—it was not far to the front lines—to encourage
the men; and upon numerous occasions I went out to bring in the
wounded or to bring in the dead. We can honestly say that there was no
wounded man who did not receive spiritual comfort from the chaplain
and, unlike some other units, there was no dead body which was not
recovered, in spite of danger and difficulty.

In addition, I was able to encourage the fighting men, and on
Sunday I went about from company to company having a psalm and a
prayer with men in exposed positions—conducting fourteen services
in all and reaching a large number of men.

While doing this I was forced by circumstances to join one company
in an attack which took us all around the enemy positions. It was not
something I would have chosen to do but, being with them, it was safer

to go on than to go back, or so I thought. The men also appreciated my presence.

Tom, my assistant, was with me, and at one time it was necessary for him to dispose of a Japanese sniper. He regretted it as much as I did, but we were exposed to his fire and there seemed no other course of action. Fortunately, perhaps, Tom is an Expert Shot with the M-1. I am recommending him for a decoration, not for this act, but for his whole conduct in the operation, which was exemplary. In earlier combat I had tried, and succeeded, in getting away from him, because I didn't want to expose him to danger. But later he protested so vigorously that I had to permit him to accompany me everywhere.

God has surely been good to me, and I only wish all the men had been as fortunate as I. All of us were mighty thankful when the job was successfully accomplished and we were able to move out last night. We only took one prisoner, but I was able to minister to him. Against the orders of a misguided and, I think, now repentant ~~officer~~ *individual*, I gave the prisoner food and water, reminding the ~~commander~~ *others* that I had my orders from a Superior who had insisted that if my enemy hungers I should feed him and if he was thirsty I should give him drink. . . .

I think that for us the worst is over so don't worry about us. Not more than you can help, anyhow.

Russell

Upon rereading the typewritten letter, Stroup attempted to blacken two words in the next-to-last paragraph and substituted other words by hand. Many years later he would explain that the commander was trying to force the prisoner to disclose enemy positions by depriving him of food and water.

By the end of that Sunday, all Japanese resistance had been overcome. "In the last two days," Robert Ross Smith reported in the official U.S. Army history, Triumph in the Philippines, *"The 1st Infantry's battalion lost approximately 20 men killed and 50 wounded while killing an additional 225 Japanese. . . . The [Japanese] Omori Detachment had indeed fought to the death" (164). The wounded were taken west to field hospital facilities in San Carlos. Stroup accompanied them and wrote the preceding letter home on Monday.*

In his notebook, Stroup listed fifteen soldiers, killed during these three days, whom he attended personally and about whom he wrote home. He also listed 102 wounded soldiers whom he visited in the San Carlos hospital: last name, company, and often a comment on their condition—"leg amputated below knee," "bad," "fractured ribs, clean wound," "amputated hand," "right arm amputated," "cast, chest & legs," "good shape," "doing well," "walked out," "back to duty."

This engagement provided a complex moral climax to Stroup's work as chaplain. He embraced a vocation, carrying the Cross, that relieved all his doubts. He trusted God's providence absolutely and served the men completely. At the same time, he was able to say for the first time, without reservation, "I think I did my part."

He retained some of his distance from the army—moral distance that derived from his religious and his pacifist convictions. He refused to defend himself. He did not surrender to hatred but loved the enemy and gave telling witness to that love by feeding a prisoner against a direct order. He retained his awareness of a transcendent ethic, even in times of great fatigue and stress.

Stroup's pattern of aggressive service could easily have led to injury or death. He would later receive a Bronze Star for his efforts on these days. The award, dated October 12, 1945, reads:

> *By direction of the President, you have been awarded the Bronze Star Medal by the Commanding General, 6th Infantry Division. The citation is as follows:*
>
> *For heroic achievement in connection with military operations against the enemy in the Cabaruan Hills, Luzon, Philippine Islands on 28 January 1945. Upon his own initiative, Captain Stroup, a chaplain attached to the infantry battalion, circulated among the assault units, administering last rites to the dying and bringing comfort to the wounded. With total disregard for his own safety, he personally assisted with the evacuation of many of the wounded men. Captain Stroup's actions reflect high credit upon himself and are deserving of high praise.*

Later that January week, Stroup rejoined his battalion, which had continued its southward march to Cuyapo, fifteen miles southeast of the Cabaruan Hills. On Friday night the battalion was ordered to force-march due east toward hills held by the Japanese 2d Tank Division. Stroup wrote in his diary, "All night march from Cuyapo to below Muñoz and San Jose, to cut supply road. Radio telling [me], Report to GHQ [General Headquarters] 6th Army. Ride in jeep."

When he reached headquarters on Saturday afternoon, February 3, he received orders from the assistant secretary of war to return immediately to Washington. The order was accompanied by a "highest priority" transportation clearance, normally reserved for generals and dignitaries. Officers demanded to know, "Who are you, anyway?" but Stroup was just as baffled by his orders as they.

On Sunday he flew to the air base at Leyte, farther south in the Philippine Archipelago. He flew on Tuesday from Leyte to Guam, on Wednesday from Guam to Hawaii, and on Wednesday night from Hawaii to the mainland, arriving in San Francisco on the morning of Thursday, February 8. Somewhere along this route he was able to secure a clean uniform and discard his dirt-and-blood-stained fatigues.

I remember my uncle describing what he felt when he reached San Francisco. He walked the combat-free hills, lost and devastated. His heart and his imagination remained in a world far more real to him, where soldiers still needed him. He did not quickly recover.

Postscript
"The Burden of the Cross"

An elderly relative reminded me of an incident when Stroup first returned to Lynchburg. The family's loyal cocker spaniel, General Robert E. Lee, had watched over Emma with particular care during Stroup's absence, sleeping outside her bedroom door every night. When General saw and smelled his master again, he went into a paroxysm of joy, running and leaping for half an hour. Then the old dog retreated to an empty room and slept for several days.

After his return, it took Stroup six weeks to recover his composure. It was not until Sunday, April 1, that he stepped behind the pulpit of the First Presbyterian Church in Lynchburg to address his congregation. Because he remained on active duty with the army, he preached in his dress uniform, recounting some of his experiences and sharing some of his feelings. Several church members who were present on that day have assured me that there was "not a dry eye in the congregation."

After that, Stroup rarely spoke of his war experiences in public, although he did share some stories with friends. Throughout the remainder of his life he studied the writings of Abraham Lincoln and Robert E. Lee, men whose faith was challenged by the necessities of combat, and he drew insights from them in his sermons. Once, at a Memorial Day service, Stroup took his old pocket notebook into the pulpit and read the names of men he had buried in the Philippines— those to whom this book is dedicated. His tears on that day were again shared by many.

On February 15, a week after his arrival in San Francisco, Stroup reported to the office of the assistant secretary of war in Washington, D.C. Friends recall that shortly thereafter Stroup was introduced to

General George C. Marshall, then chief of staff of the U.S. Army. Stroup treasured the memory of this visit with a man whom he considered both great and kind. When he asked the general about the fate of his unit in the Philippines, Marshall ordered that Stroup be taken to the Pentagon map room to be briefed on the campaign he had left two weeks earlier.

Stroup was initially assigned to the office of the assistant secretary of war as "liaison officer and writer," according to his subsequent Separation Record. On May 31 he was transferred to the office of the chief of chaplains but continued similar work with the "Special Planning Division, O.S.S." On June 13, he was promoted to major. Some mystery surrounds these assignments, but my recollections—based upon family conversations—are that the army had ordered Stroup to the Pentagon in order to assist a liaison project with American churches. As the war drew to a close, the army wished to persuade the public to accept a continuation into peacetime of "universal military training"—the code phrase of the day—for all young men of draft age. Senior officers had heard that Stroup favored universal military training and, because he was a Protestant chaplain with an outstanding record in combat and a gift for both writing and speaking, they hoped he might play a role in this campaign.

Stroup did indeed favor a form of universal military training, but it was not what the army advocated. As he indicated in his letter of December 15, 1944, Stroup had come to admire the "citizen-soldier," but his distrust of military professionals remained. He hoped that, with the end of hostilities, America might largely disband its professional army but continue to train all young men against a possible emergency— rather like the modern Swiss army reserves, or the citizen-militia of the American colonies that mobilized to support the Revolution. He saw this as a strategy to remove from American society the threat of militarism while providing for national protection in emergencies. The army, on the other hand, anticipated the continuation of a large, technologically advanced, standing army overseeing deep reserves of civilians trained for combat.

As it turned out, both the army and Stroup lost an important opportunity. If he had been asked to lecture at the Army War College on morale and ethics in combat, or assigned to review the curriculum at schools for the training of chaplains, or given time to edit these letters for publication, Stroup might have been able to use his own experiences to offer creative insights for improving the training and deployment of chaplains. As it was, there is no evidence that Stroup pursued his assignment to flack for the army with any enthusiasm, although his discharge records indicate that he "Received letters of commendation from . . . Commanding General, Special Planning Division, Special Staff." As far as I can determine, Stroup—so prolific a writer from the combat zone—published nothing during this period, nor is there evidence that he addressed any church organizations about the army training plan.

The Germans surrendered that summer. In October, Stroup received his Bronze Star, and during that fall he was able more frequently to spend the weekend at his church in Lynchburg. He was relieved from active military duty on December 23, 1945, and returned to his congregation full time. He was honorably discharged from the U.S. Army in February 1946.

In his letters, Stroup frequently referred to the unusual protection of Providence. He appreciated escaping unharmed from one dangerous situation after another, but the reality meant more to him than that. Providence was not, for Stroup, a sense that his time was appointed and therefore he was safe until that day arrived. His sense of Providence drew from the Wesleyan piety of his Methodist heritage. It was rooted in his sensory awareness of the presence of a God who was no abstraction but a daily companion. He grew up in a household where God's presence was palpable, and he drank deeply from that well of common experience. Divine presence offered a continual dialogue of choice and response. If God rescued Stroup from one danger, it was because God had another task for him among the men to whom he was assigned. Stroup, in turn, had to choose over and again to respond to God's apparent purpose for him in the circumstances of combat.

Providence was not simply protection but an assured intermingling of time and "eternity"—one of Stroup's favorite words. His memories of his own father, who had died when he was nine years old yet remained a strong influence in the family, suggested that the eternity of God's people continued nearby. Although Stroup was a sophisticated intellectual in an age when other thinkers limited their universe to the boundaries defined by science, for him Heaven remained a palpable, sociable place of joyful reunion, just a step beyond the grave. This conviction robbed death of much of its sting and made more sensible a courage that might otherwise appear foolhardy.

Stroup was not an evangelist, as his mother had been in her younger days. He was deeply committed to free inquiry and resisted any form of manipulation of the minds of others, even for the most holy purpose. Therefore, to share his strong faith and convictions, he adopted a strategy quite different from evangelistic persuasion. His approach was to become an example—and then respond to questions. He could not simply be a chaplain; he must become a soldier. Preaching, teaching, and comforting the afflicted would remain hollow, he was convinced, until the soldiers knew that Stroup shared their lot and surpassed them in bravery. Then, and only then, would they ask him questions and ponder his responses. We have observed this dialogue build as Stroup achieved a reputation among soldiers and officers alike. On his last days in combat, Stroup expanded his role until the boundary between time and eternity nearly dissolved as Stroup became foolhardy or transcendent—the reader must decide. I am grateful that at this point Providence removed my uncle from battle, although he resented the transfer, and the army did not benefit from it.

While closely identifying himself with the troops, Stroup maintained a posture that distinguished him from army culture. He refused to become an army flack. The most visible symbol of this separateness was his determination to enter combat unarmed. Many other chaplains declined to bear arms, but few of them undertook infantry training and then volunteered for frequent front-line missions. Stroup's posture was distinctive, shared only by the conscientious objectors who performed brave alternative service as medics. Because his choices were voluntary, and because he was an officer, they carried particular weight.

Stroup's unarmed presence also served to remind soldiers that he was among them to represent a different authority. He witnessed to a source of security stronger than that provided by guns and an authority higher than the military chain of command. On rare occasions he boldly invoked that authority. Stroup's unarmed presence was not a judgment upon the soldiers' task. He respected what they were required by circumstances to do. Indeed, as Stroup wrote in *Harper's*, the soldiers' obligation "to shoot, stab, and throttle their enemies" was part of the burden of the cross carried by men drafted into a conflict they had not created. "They long to understand the reason for the cross on which they hang and that other Cross where goodness, justice, mercy, beauty, honor, and love are crucified." Killing was as dangerous to the soul as was death to the body. The antidote was a knowledge of God's forgiveness and a spirit of compassion large enough to embrace even the enemy. These kept the soul alive.

At Hollandia, after his first week in combat, Stroup preached on Jesus' hard saying, "Ye have heard that it was said . . . Thou shalt not kill . . . But I say unto you, That whosoever is angry with his brother . . . shall be in danger of the judgement" (Matt. 5:21, 22). Following that sermon Stroup spent evenings in no-man's-land, unarmed and alone in his jeep, in the hope that some Japanese soldier might be encouraged to surrender. None did, but one of Stroup's hearers, surprised by such a Japanese soldier, found the courage to receive him. Stroup and a medic knelt before "Charlie" to wash his sores. Even though the soldier reminded them that his job had been to kill Americans, Stroup's unit accepted Charlie. So a circle of redemption was completed.

Stroup's combat pacifism was a unique spiritual insight that he sought to impart both by example and by teaching. While condemning the evils of war and recognizing the threat that killing posed to the human spirit, Stroup under fire fashioned strategies of redemption to rescue the souls of participants and to limit the carnage. He helped the soldiers carry their cross.

Stroup's superior officers valued him for the positive effect he had on troop morale. Soldiers who overcame excessive fear, who became more confident, courageous, and caring of one another, would form a safer unit as well as a more effective one. Yet, if the quality of chaplaincy that Stroup exemplified had become more widespread, field commanders would have had to reckon with an alternative moral authority in their midst. The results would have been difficult, but possibly salutary for the future of the armed forces.

As Stroup pointed out in his articles for home consumption, it was not simply the army's fault that chaplains could be ineffectual flacks and moral flunkies. The fault lay as much with the churches that supplied them. They provided no coherent theology and discipline of the chaplaincy—whether in the military, in hospitals, in prisons, or elsewhere—that might inspire chaplains to bond with those they served and to resist co-optation by the institutions within which they functioned.

Although Stroup, in combat, always remained the servant of a higher power, he came in time to identify more with the army and less with the church. In his principal message to the American public, "A Soldier Looks at the Church," he wrote as a Christian soldier. He had bonded with a new congregation: the community of those who, regardless of creed or denomination, shared risk on the front lines of life. Deprived of the routines of home and faced with a common danger, members of the "1st Battalion" had more in common with each other than did members of "First Presbyterian." A pastor whom they trusted could help them all to grow in spirit. This, for Stroup, was the finest evangelism. He would later look for similar opportunities in a long and distinguished civilian pastoral ministry. But when death from cancer approached in 1977, Stroup's seventy-second year, this Christian pacifist asked to be buried in his army dress uniform. He remembered his year in combat as his finest ministry.

I believe that my uncle would not want me to prescribe his pattern as a model for Christian ministry or chaplaincy. He would want us to reflect upon it, to ask our own questions, and to search our own souls.

Although Stroup rarely referred to his war experiences from the pulpit, he did preach often from a favorite text, Matthew 16:24–26:

> Then said Jesus unto his disciples, If any man will come after me, let him deny himself, and take up his cross, and follow me.
>
> For whosoever will save his life shall lose it: and whosoever will lose his life for my sake shall find it.
>
> For what is a man profited, if he shall gain the whole world, and lose his own soul? or what shall a man give in exchange for his soul?

Acknowledgments

Although several military histories were consulted in the preparation of this book, the most useful proved to be the official histories published by the Department of the Army and written by Robert Ross Smith: *The Approach to the Philippines* (1953; rpt. Washington, D.C.: Center of Military History, U.S. Army, 1996) and *Triumph in the Philippines* (1963; rpt. Washington, D.C.: Center of Military History, U.S. Army, 1993). The maps included herein have been taken from these volumes, as has much of the information provided about the troop movements.

Excerpts from "A Soldier Looks at the Church," published in the October 1944 issue of *Harper's Magazine*, along with comments by the editors published in that issue, and the cover of that issue, have been used by permission.

Excerpts from "Fear in the Shadows," published in 1944, have been used by permission of the *Presbyterian Outlook.*

The editor acknowledges a particular debt to Jeff Price, the nephew of Russell Stroup's wife, Louise, who uncovered the letters in the house occupied by Russell and Louise and then by his mother, Marie Price. I also thank Carol Musgrave and Terese Austin for their research assistance. Photographs and other materials used to illustrate this book were retained by Stroup's mother and by his wife and were given to me by Louise Stroup during her lifetime.

In his 1944 Christmas letter to his family, Stroup wrote, "If Richard were a bit older I'd try to help him understand what he means to us all, and to me. He is 'our immortality.'" Through tragic circumstance, I remain the only surviving heir of Stroup and of all the family members to whom that letter was addressed.

Russell Cartwright Stroup's manuscript letters and all other family materials used in the preparation of this book—and in the preparation of two additional books drawing from the Stroup family legacy—have been deposited with the Stroup Family Papers at the Western Reserve Historical Society, Cleveland, Ohio.

Index